The popularity of using narrative, metaphor and building solutions in cognitive behavioural therapy (CBT) has increased in recent years. Narrative CBT (NCBT), part of the third wave of cognitive therapies, recognizes the importance of helping to build new ideas and practices in order to create change, examining a person's multiple and evolving narratives and his or her behaviour as intrinsically meaningful.

In *Narrative CBT*, John Rhodes presents the features of NCBT in thirty key points. The first fifteen summarize how the theory of narrative can clarify difficulties with emotions, motives and interactions and address how rebuilding confidence and trust is crucial for change to be achieved. In the second half of the book, case conceptualization and the techniques of NCBT are explained and illustrated. Narrative, solution-oriented and CBT techniques are integrated and specific NCBT approaches for trauma, depression and obsessive-compulsive disorder are highlighted.

Ideal for clinical and counselling psychologists, both established and in training, psychotherapists and all professionals carrying out therapy in the field of mental health, this book clearly and accessibly presents the techniques and key concepts of Narrative CBT.

John Rhodes is a consultant clinical psychologist in the NHS, working with clients diagnosed as having psychoses, long-term mood disorders and traumas. He is a visiting lecturer at the University of Hertfordshire and Honorary Lecturer at University College London. He has previously co-authored *Solution Focused Thinking in Schools* and *Narrative CBT for Psychosis*.

Cognitive behavioural therapy (CBT) occupies a central position in the move towards evidence-based practice and is frequently used in the clinical environment. Yet there is no one universal approach to CBT and clinicians speak of first-, second- and even third-wave approaches.

This series provides straightforward, accessible guides to a number of CBT methods, clarifying the distinctive features of each approach. The series editor, Windy Dryden, successfully brings together experts from each discipline to summarize the 30 main aspects of their approach divided into theoretical and practical features.

The CBT Distinctive Features Series will be essential reading for psychotherapists, counsellors and psychologists of all orientations who want to learn more about the range of new and developing cognitive behavioural approaches.

Titles in the series:

For further information about this series please visit www.routledgementalhealth.com/cbt-distinctive-features

Narrative CBT

Distinctive Features

John Rhodes

Routledge
Taylor & Francis Group

LONDON AND NEW YORK

First published 2014
by Routledge
27 Church Road, Hove, East Sussex BN3 2FA

Simultaneously published in the USA and Canada
by Routledge
711 Third Avenue, New York, NY 10017

*Routledge is an imprint of the Taylor & Francis Group,
an informa business*

British Library Cataloguing in Publication Data
A catalogue record for this book is available from the British
Library

Library of Congress Cataloging in Publication Data
A catalog record for this book has been requested

ISBN: 978-0-415-53396-6 (hbk)
ISBN: 978-0-415-53397-3 (pbk)
ISBN: 978-1-315-88505-6 (ebk)

Typeset in Times
by Swales & Willis Ltd, Exeter, Devon

Printed and bound in the United States of America by Publishers Graphics,
LLC on sustainably sourced paper.

Contents

Acknowledgements

I would like to thank for their help and contributions: Peter Howson, Annupama Rammohan, Luke Bosdet, Jayne Tinney and Richard Gipps. Also thanks to Windy Dryden for inviting me to write this book, and Joanne Forshaw and Susannah Frearson at Routledge.

Abbreviations

CBT	cognitive behavioural therapy
COMET	competitive memory training
DSM	*Diagnostic and Statistical Manual of Mental Disorders*
NCBT	narrative cognitive behavioural therapy
NSF	narrative and solution-focused
NSFT	narrative and solution-focused therapies
OCD	obsessive-compulsive disorder
PCT	personal construct theory
SF	solution-focused
SFT	solution-focused therapy

Part 1

THE DISTINCTIVE THEORETICAL FEATURES OF NARRATIVE CBT

1

Introduction to NCBT

One aim of this book is to explore how narrative ideas and practices can be combined with selected aspects of cognitive behavioural therapy (CBT) and I will term such approaches narrative CBT (NCBT). Narrative as a way of understanding psychological phenomena is also a theme that runs through the whole book. I will cover approaches that in a direct way help the client to narrate past difficult events, as in types of work with trauma. I will also greatly draw on narrative and solution-focused therapies (NSFT) which provide not only ways of narrating the past, but to a great extent emphasize narrating and building new ideas, practices and possible futures, that is, it aims to be 'constructional'. This was always a key idea in de Shazer's (1988) description of SFT, but was also central for White and Epston's (1990) narrative therapy, which aims at the building of a benign new conception of identity and way of living.

Whilst there is a focus on narrative, the book will also emphasize other aspects of mind and self, in particular, the central importance of feelings, motivations, trust and complex interaction. All these features are relevant to everyday life, but also to forms of suffering, and finding ways of change. The importance of interaction has always been a part of NSFT, which had its origin in systemic therapy. NCBT is the critical fusion of compatible practices and theory from classic CBT with NSFT.

A brief definition of CBT

Roughly speaking, CBT could be defined as therapy that works with conscious meanings and also works to change behaviours. CBT itself

3

is an integration of the original behavioural approaches with cognitive ones. CBT has, however, several schools of thought (Dryden, 2012). For many CBT practitioners the cognition or belief is central to explanation and change, but this is not the case for some older and more recent behaviourists.

Conceptual recourses for NCBT

In this section I wish to outline briefly some general psychological, and in fact sometimes philosophical, assumptions, theories and themes that are relevant to the version of NCBT present in this book. Some ideas will be touched on again, but space does not allow further detailed discussion of all these ideas.

Constructivism

One general resource to draw on is that of ideas and theories from constructivist psychology and the humanities. The term 'constructivism' is very broad. For the purpose of this book I will take constructivism to be approaches that have emphasized how meaning is central to explaining and understanding human experience and, furthermore, that people engage in the active making of meaning in a multitude of ways (Mahoney, 1991, 2003). This approach is therefore not classic behaviourism, but neither is it an approach to the mind using explanation by computer models and so-called 'information processing', as seems to be assumed in many forms of cognitive psychology. The emphasis is, rather, on topics such as the everyday use of language, interaction, negotiation of meaning and the influence of culture.

The narrative mind

A great deal of mental phenomena has the nature of being 'literate' (Bruner, 1986; Turner, 1996); that is to say that a fundamental feature of the mind is that it can generate stories and metaphors, and that the use of these is central, pervasive and perhaps unavoidable. However, whilst narrative is central, some have argued that it may well depend for its emergence or characteristics on early prenarrative experience of the body, perception and features of interaction (Gallagher, 2007).

Interaction and the self

It will be argued that we need better and more complex concepts of behaviour than are usually used in CBT if we wish to understand human interaction. We need to think in terms of purposeful actions, but also to consider the role of habitual ways of interacting which emerge spontaneously in specific situations. Of course, theories of 'behaviour' were once the very living heart of behaviourism. However, after the emergence of cognitive therapy, somehow what behaviour might actually be tended to be ignored or forgotten.

Critical realism

Following philosophers such as Searle (1992), I will assume there is a 'mind independent reality', however difficult, or sometimes impossible, it is to know. In addition, usually with clients we need to assume some everyday notion of 'truth', of what has 'really happened'. Has the person undergone the oppression of racism and other prejudices? What are the real effects of growing up in poverty or war? I do not believe such effects are just a matter of 'how you view things'.

This book does not therefore assume complete 'relativity' as some writers on narrative have appeared to do (Bruner, 1986). I find more convincing the ideas of critical realism that our theories are influenced by cultural and historic factors. However, that does not prevent an attempt at objectivity, or of sharing evidence, or of exploring clients' real contexts and experiences. We need, however, to be aware of our own theories, of how we bring our own limited ideas to a phenomenon. Our conceptualizations of clients' difficulties need to be very modest and cautious.

Many levels of explanation

For any phenomena such as anxiety or delusions, many 'levels' of explanation could be relevant, depending on the purpose in hand. Neuropsychology, quantitative psychology and the sociology of groups can all play a role. However, in our face-to-face therapeutic work perhaps the greatest need is to understand the immediate experiences of the person in his or her lived world, and for that we also need to draw on qualitative psychology and related topics in the humanities.

Philosophy of mind and phenomenology

At several points I will draw upon ideas from phenomenology and philosophy. In recent decades there has been a lot of philosophical work concerning areas such as narrative, emotions and interaction, and these, I believe, can help our thinking in psychology.

Following certain philosophers, I will assume that mental phenomena are characterized by 'intentionality', that mental phenomena are 'directed', are 'about' things, and that concepts such as belief, desire and decision are real aspects of the mind (Searle, 1983; Gallagher and Zahavi, 2008). Whilst these everyday terms have diverse meanings (Ratcliffe, 2007), I believe they are clearer than many alternatives in psychology such as the concept of 'information processing', a term much used but rarely defined.

The history of NCBT

Some in the CBT tradition have drawn heavily on constructivism and developmental psychology, in particular Guidano and Liotti (1983), and later Mahoney (1991, 2003). Guidano and Liotti suggested that core beliefs or 'tacit knowledge' concerning world and self may develop from types of attachment situation in childhood, and drew on the work of Bowlby (1969). As part of their therapy, they suggested repeated focus on key moments in the past, one aim being to develop a richer narrative and new understanding of what had really taken place, in contrast to a person's distorted explanations. Mahoney emphasized how a person might have not only a specific problem, but a problem pattern over years and core processes that organize experience: for long-term patterns he suggested the use of a life review. All of these therapists used a form of narrative in their therapy in combination with the use of CBT.

Narrative- and solution-orientated therapy developed completely independently of CBT: certain CBT therapists, however, noticed deep similarities between CBT and NSFT and went on to suggest various types of fusion of practice and theory: such writers include Russell (1991), Meichenbaum (1993, 1994), Gonçalves (1994), Ramsay (1998) and, more recently, Hallam and O'Connor (2002), Griffin (2003), Postma and Rao (2006), Rhodes and Jakes (2009) and Bannick (2012).

Whilst there are many differences between CBT and NSFT, there are strong similarities and compatibilities such that I believe the two can make a coherent and practical fusion. Some key similarities are:

1. Both emphasize the role of accessible or conscious meaning and how transformation of meaning is central (Brewin and Power, 1999).
2. Both underline the role of 'behaviour' and interaction in real-world contexts. Furthermore, that change usually involves changes in 'behaviour', or, as White might say, in taking new 'initiatives'.

Outline of the book

In the theory part of the book I will first examine selected key features of human experience or mind which are relevant in attempting to understand a person for the purpose of therapy (for example, narrative, metaphors or interactions). At the same time, a view of pathology will be outlined drawing on these concepts. The later theory chapters will look at how various aspects of NCBT might work with particular relevance to how narrative and constructional ideas might produce change. Part 2 illustrates a variety of NCBT techniques, looks at how to plan work and will illustrate the distinctive use of NCBT for complex presentations of depression, obsessive-compulsive disorder, trauma and social difficulties.

2

Narrative

If you ask a patient what was happening before depression started, then you are quite likely to hear a complex emotional narrative of negative events and suffering. If you later ask how that person would like to live, then, with some difficulty, you might hear the person construct an outline of a better way of living. There is sometimes articulated an outline of how one thing might change and then another: in short, a narrative of a possible future. Listening carefully, one might also notice subtle metaphors or analogies (e.g. it felt like the end of my world), complex visual images and quoted dialogue from the past.

Human experience and expression are permeated by narrative and other complex linguistic forms (dialogues, explanations and discourse). In the therapy room narrative is a key focus. Of course, we also observe, perceive and feel as we interact with the person (Ratcliffe, 2007), yet these too cohere and add to the flow of narrative.

Given this ubiquity of narrative, then it is not surprising that various ways of using narrative have emerged in different therapies, including the practice of CBT.

A great number of writers have stressed the central importance of narrative for understanding features of human experience: for example, MacIntyre (1981), Ricoeur (1984), Bruner (1986), Sarbin (1986), Hutto (2008). All have stressed how our thinking and lives are permeated by narrative and that narrative is found in everyday life and not only in novels and films.

Some writers in fact suggest that forms of narrative, as found in play or song, are observed in the very earliest interactions of infant and carer (Trevarthan and Aitkin, 2001). Turner (1996) also suggests that our minds are literate from the beginning and that artistic forms in adulthood develop from the basic abilities of our early years.

Self-constitution and narrative

Some theorists have gone further and suggest that a person's very 'self' is created in the act of narration or, rather, that as the person grows up, the act of narrating is engaged in repeatedly until a self is formed. This extreme position has, however, received strong criticism: Zahavi (2007) argues that there is a sort of basic and continuous consciousness that engages in narration and, following Damasio (1999), argues for the notion of a 'core consciousness' and core self, as opposed to what he termed 'extended consciousness' and an autobiographical self. Damasio gives several arguments for this position, including the observation that some patients lose their memory for the past yet are still conscious in the present. However, in thinking about this issue, we can also simply ask: what is it that narrates the self? How could the process start without some elementary consciousness?

Gallagher (2007) has argued that the capacity to narrate in fact depends on other capacities and suggests four: an ability to order events in time; a minimal sense of self, for example, that I know it was me that began a phone call, and me that ended it; having autobiographic memories; and a metacognitive ability to reflect on the content. He also argues, as stated, for the emergence of narrative in the context of our ability to interact and feel.

This book is compatible with either theory of the self: the essential upshot is, however, that persons in quiet reflection, but also in the heat of the moment, engage in telling the stories of their lives, and these conceptualizations involve ideas on events but also complex pictures of what a person is. The stories show a person as strong or weak, liked or disliked, with a future or without, and so on. And of course, this process involves multiple, sometimes conflicting, stories of the self in a social context where we are also 'narrated' by others, that is, we may hear stories about ourselves which in turn influence our development.

It is sometimes useful in therapy to isolate a key thought or belief such as 'no one likes me', yet these specific thoughts are almost always deeply connected to evolving stories of the self and stories of life itself. For example, how someone could not find work after taking a bold risk or how someone loses contact with a child in a divorce. It might be better to think of stark self-belief statements as conclusions of stories.

We tell stories of our lives, but a consequence of this might be that the story itself then begins to structure the development of a life. If we believe, as one client did, that 'whenever a good thing has happened, then a bad thing follows', and this person can narrate several examples, then we are likely to avoid all new things and never accept any positive change. The assumption of narrative influence was always central to White and Epston's work (1990).

Does 'life' itself have 'narrative' structure?

Goldie (2004) argues that life itself has narrative structure: that is, our everyday lives involve unfolding events in time, and really do, for example, involve journeys, struggles, finding, losing, success and failure and leaving home and coming home. The content and structure of our narrative, the telling of story and drama, imitate the nature of real life.

Perhaps a modest middle position might be that while much of life seems 'contingent', chance-like, without obvious 'beginning' and 'end', some aspects of life do have a pattern (birth and death), and sometimes there are complex unfolding sequences (for example, falling in love). Narrative in the end might emerge from our lived practices of being in the world.

Other expressive forms

I have spoken particularly of 'narrative', yet also importantly, there are other related forms such as remembered dialogues and discursive actions such as promising, explaining or 'accounting' for something (Harré, 1979). All these may be of relevance to therapy and exploring the internal dialogue of a person might be particularly useful for some problems (Hallam and O'Connor, 2002).

In short, narrative is central in everyday talk and indispensable in therapy. Its presence may not be emphasized in classic CBT yet it is a notion compatible with concepts of core belief or automatic thoughts and adds richness to therapeutic work. In this book, narrative is conceived as the alternative to specific cognitions.

Problems with narration

Gallagher (2007) suggests there can be two major types of difficulty with narrative: 'content' versus 'structure'. Giving structure or shape to stories might be thought of as the capacity to narrate. At its most extreme, in neurological problems, the person loses the capacity to tell any type of coherent narrative, such as what happened that morning. Other patients, in particular those in the middle of a psychotic breakdown, seem to become very confused, and any recounting of events is difficult to follow.

Narrative content presents with many difficulties. White and Epston (1990) coined the famous phrase 'problem-saturated story'. The person arrives in therapy and can only talk of problems, losses and failure. Nothing else seems to exist. At the opposite end, however, one can think of clients who suffer due to the non-telling of their stories, such as clients who quickly say they had a happy childhood, yet also mention serious family disruption and difficulty. And perhaps a middle position is that of posttraumatic stress disorder, where fragments of memories return repeatedly, yet are not put into a coherent whole.

O'Connor et al. (2006) argued that narrative by its very nature tends to be persuasive, to capture our imagination, and it achieves this by the power of its integrated structure, its emphasis on connection of events over time, vivid dialogue, metaphors, and so on. The 'unit' of the whole story is difficult to challenge by specific facts. More likely to succeed is the building of a credible alternative story.

Narrative and pathologies

There is a growing literature on narrative and its role in different kinds of pathology. However, there is only space to mention one or two illustrative examples.

Rhodes and Smith (2010) described a single case of situational depression: it was striking from the man's account how, during the actual period of breakdown, under the onslaught of financial problems, this man began to renarrate his life. He said that over the course of three weeks, all the 'dark stuff' came into his mind, memories of all the negative things he had ever done. We described this as a catastrophic renarration. Ridge (2009) has studied narratives of 'recovery' in depression, how clients succeeded or not in making sense of their years of suffering.

Narrative is just as much about character as about events. Clients regularly add to their stories comments such as 'I'm useless' or even 'I am evil'. Sometimes they begin with such banner headline comments, then proceed to illustrate them with the description of episodes.

Stories also contain vivid metaphors which clients quite spontaneously add: 'after this happened, I felt like a child'. As stated, narrative and metaphor may both describe and contribute to suffering: in one piece of research (Rhodes and Jakes, 2004) we noted how some metaphors used about specific experiences in the past had then become part of a person's ongoing experience such that over time the origins of the metaphor were lost. For example, before a breakdown a person may say he or she feels 'like I am dead', but in full psychosis say 'I am dead'.

A key focus of therapy can be to explore stories and metaphors, both those of suffering, but also those of strengths and hopes. The aim in NCBT is not just to question cognitions, but to question negative stories and often to help build more benign narratives of self.

3

Metaphors

Metaphors are vivid expressions and creations of thoughts and feelings: if we listen in therapy, clients can be heard to use them to express powerful ideas and feelings of how they experience the world. While beautiful or striking, they can also be painful and distressing, as we shall see later, and they might even in themselves add to a person's continued suffering.

There are many ways of describing different types of figures of speech, but I will discuss, drawing on Lakoff (1987; Lakoff and Johnson, 1980), mainly metaphors and sometimes metonymy. Following Lakoff, I will assume metaphor to be in fact a variation of analogy. Of course, definitions of these can be difficult, but for this book I will suggest the following:

*   Metaphors often involve some type of comparison, or at least, associated link between two 'domains' or conceptual areas ('Juliet is the sun').
*   In metonymy, we use a part of a conceptual domain to stand for the whole ('we need a new pair of hands around here'). We can use part for whole, but also whole for part ('are you on the network?').

The following are just a few metaphors I've heard in recent therapy.

*   I feel like a dead person.
*   I am a waste of space.
*   I am scum.

One can use metaphor to explore how someone feels, often in ways literal language does not capture, but one can also use metaphors to think of preferred states or goals for the future. In a later chapter I will explore how one can work therapeutically with such examples. I shall now explore some further aspects of metaphor and how this relates to therapy.

Core metaphors of oneself

A core metaphor could be a statement such as 'I am a fool' and in extreme cases the person might make a repeated claim such as 'I am a freak' or worse.

Here we see some of the power of metaphor used against the person: the statement is harsh, extreme, distressing and suggestive of scenarios of being looked down upon, of being an object of disgust, and yet such statements are 'vague' and open to many interpretations. The fact they are so vague makes them difficult to disprove by direct evidence.

Blends

A development in recent years of the theory of metaphor and related categories has been the concept of the 'blend' (Fauconnier and Turner, 2002). A metaphor is a simple blend, but a complex blend is the fusion of several elements or areas of meaning to create something new, such as a 'robot', or even impossible, such as a talking animal. Such blended creations are often found in literature. As we talk, however, it is not unusual for a person to use a complex blended scenario to explain or express an idea. For example, we can imagine what one philosopher from ancient times might say to someone living now.

In Rhodes and Smith (2010), the following was noted in the talk of a depressed man: on receipt of a dreaded remortgage letter, he said out loud: 'Bye bye life'. This is not just a metaphor: his 'life' is seen as a house and its loss as a death. It also implies a story of achieving and losing and anticipating a bleak future.

Metaphoric reactions

There are certain problematic situations clients face where the actual experience, in particular the quality of the feeling, seems to have what I think of as real yet metaphoric quality. For example, one client said that when in a situation where she fears abandonment, she feels as if she might 'stop existing', that is, that she might really disappear. This was an intelligent non-psychotic client. This is not just a way of expressing herself at the time, using an intentional metaphor, and the client was not just trying to express her experience vividly for me.

Another client told me spontaneously that when he sees a woman attacked on TV, then 'I am sitting in that place'. He went on to underline the strangeness of the experience yet that he knew he was not the woman or like a woman. He had been the object of repeated domestic violence and watching this seemed to bring back a sort of reliving process where he felt he was that victim.

Perhaps our reactions, our perceptions of difficult events, are made of many levels and associations. Some are upfront and clear: for example, fear of attack by a dog. Yet intermingled with this are expectations formed in the past, memories and imaginative scenarios. Some of our everyday reactions might well contain both 'real' and 'unreal' elements, but the latter, as it were, almost evaporate the second we think about our experience. They are like an aura which cannot withstand close scrutiny, yet do affect our reactions. Articulation of these can sometimes be useful in deconstructing puzzling reactions.

Metaphoric reactions, what in fact could also be thought of as 'blended reactions', might form part of extreme and hard-to-understand emotional and social reactions. If we reject a simplistic distinction between the conscious and the non-conscious, as do Talvitie and Tiitinen (2006), then perhaps the fact that some part of our experience is metaphorical, half in and half out of full consciousness, can be better understood.

Overview

If Lakoff is correct, our daily categories of thought and everyday language are composed of metaphoric and metonymic models, in addition to literal propositions, and image schemas (e.g. the image of a spiral). To explore a person's reaction in full these diverse aspects and strands can be investigated.

Lakoff suggests that metaphors are not random: rather, the metaphors a person gives are structured by the person's cultural and biophysical experiences. Generating metaphors draws upon a person's experience of living and reveals personal knowledge of how the world, self and others are experienced and understood. Metaphors are often meaning-rich in a way the communicator does not at first realize. We have metaphors in narrative, but perhaps we can also have a sort of direct metaphoric or blended experience.

4

Emotions and feelings

This chapter explores the topics of emotion and feeling with particular reference to narrative and therapy.

Narrative and emotion

Goldie (2000) argued that to understand why a person has a specific emotional reaction such as fear, or a longer-term state of being fearful, then an illuminating way of doing this is to see the emotion in the context of the person's history. For example, I am fearful now as I approach opening certain types of tin can due to a nasty accident some years ago. My reaction now makes sense in view of this history. Of course, sometimes, for example, when being barked at by a ferocious dog, we assume no history is needed in order to understand the reaction: but even here, we may need to explain why one person is more upset than others and often this relates to the history of that person.

Take a long-established couple and there can be observed an apparently neutral topic, such as a discussion on how to look after the garden, where strong emotions are expressed which can seem incomprehensible to the visitor. In such a case we can hypothesize that there has been a history of disputes.

Around any topic, any specific feature of our lives, there can be a history of actual reactions, but also a network of associations, ideas and narratives of past involvements: often we do not think about these many layers, yet they 'permeate' our responses.

Sometimes, however, the interplay of narrative and emotion is very conspicuous: in the very midst of unfolding events, the person can move in and out of telling a narrative, and a narrative of both the past and future. As a friend and I struggled to drive to our hotel at night, lost in a foreign country, for some seconds I began to ask myself 'what if we really just can't find it?' I began to imagine a future 'story' or scenario of being lost in the city, of sleeping in the car, or worse. And all the time this developing narrative was infused with a vague and growing dread.

When clients have been traumatized, or experienced great difficulties, then often the event is thought about again and again, generating many narratives of what happened, or should have happened, or might have happened. Often the narrative contains a severe negative character judgement.

We live in time and narrate the past and the future: the stories we generate can in turn influence how we act and react. To understand in therapy a person's reactions, why that person is so fearful of others, or so without hope about finding a new job, then we need to grasp the person's many narratives. We need to grasp the subjective first-person perspective of how the story is told, and we might also need to wonder about the 'untold' story, the unnarrated, the events that have occurred or are occurring and which lie outside the easy-to-access story. Some of these details might be negative, yet, as we shall see later, might also be positive.

Many of the reactions we work with in therapy are ones that have developed over many years and some of these go back to earliest childhood: these responses were created in multiple interactions. The child forms a repertoire of emotional expectations, and brings these into adult interactions. In short-term therapy one would not normally look at origins, but the latter is often needed in longer work. Sometimes a present reaction seems incomprehensible, and then looking for origins is very useful.

Cognition and emotion

Beck originally suggested that we first had automatic thoughts, and then the emotion followed. I suspect very few therapists now believe this theory, at least as a complete account, and Beck himself (1995) has presented an alternative theory of simultaneous activation of emotion and thought. A great deal of research suggests there are two separate but deeply interconnected systems of emotion and cognition (LeDoux, 1998). We can and often do have emotions which do not arise from a specific thought, automatic or otherwise. The classic thought record therefore misleads us, especially if we insist on an exact thought-to-emotion connection.

However, our thoughts, both specific and complex, do influence our emotions: we can have a sudden thought that leads to fear (I've left my keys at work!), and we can use deliberate thought at least to attempt to influence our emotions, for example, by reminding ourselves that we can cope in a situation or that something is not really dangerous. In one experiment (Phelps, 2005), participants were told that seeing a blue square on a screen might produce a shock to the wrist (but none were given at all): when the squares were seen, the participants automatically had physiological reactions of fear and an increase of activity in the amygdala, as demonstrated on a brain scan. It seems, therefore, that ideas really can have direct effects on emotions, and sometimes in ways the person does not even realize. Clinical experience suggests, however, that it is easier to learn a new fear than unlearn an old one.

Emotion and feelings

If we are asked to name an emotion, then it is most likely that people will say fear, anger, sadness, joy, and they might include 'pride', 'shame'. In everyday talk, however, it is clear that there are many ways of describing 'emotions', but that we also often speak of 'feelings', for example:

- I feel ill at ease.
- I feel you're right.

Now, the latter might translate into 'I believe you are right', that is, it expresses an idea, but not the former. There really does seem to be a feeling of being ill at ease.

21

There may in fact be a huge range of feelings which are not really well described as emotions: Goldie (2000) spoke of bodily feelings. Ratcliffe (2008) suggests that some feelings could be termed 'existential feelings' in that these feelings reveal to us the nature of the world, the world as lived. Some possible examples are feeling alienated, at home, on familiar ground or lost. Ratcliffe also argues that over long periods of time we can have a feeling, but are only aware of it sometimes. These feelings do not have a precise explicit cognitive content, they are pre-reflective.

To understand some psychopathologies, we might need to understand the alterations in a person's existential feelings. In one extreme delusion, termed Cotard's, a person claims to be dead. Ratcliffe speculates on how this might relate to a fundamental alteration in feeling of the self. In research about depression, a colleague and I have noted the centrality of feeling 'empty' (Smith and Rhodes, in press). I do not think this is a metaphor: in some deep sense the self is empty of its normal feeling of being alive.

I suspect that to understand serious changes in feeling, as for emotion, we need to take a wide view and consider a person's history, for example, how that individual underwent serious losses during a period of onset of depression, but also to explore the present perception of difficulties and the sense, perhaps feeling, that the future cannot change.

The topics of emotion, feeling and narration are deeply entwined: the articulation of a person's descriptions and narratives is a fundamental part of therapy when working with these areas.

5

Motivations: their loss and reconstruction

There are many ways of describing different systems of motivation. A strong contribution has been made by the ideas of Gilbert (1989), who suggests that there are certain fundamental motivations: to give care, be cared for, to co-operate and engage in competition (he acknowledges others such as sexual desire). He argues these derive from evolved biosocial mentalities and are shared with other mammals. Based on an analysis of narratives, McAdams (1993) suggested two main motives, that of intimacy and of power. In contrast to both, Baumeister (2005) gives an extremely open list of motivations combining physical, social and cultural needs and desires. His list includes control, power and food, belongingness, sex, nurturance, self-esteem, the desire to be moral, and for a meaningful life.

For the type of therapy described in this book, there is no need to attempt to decide which system is the correct one, and anyway, I suspect that most of these systems overlap. However, what is crucial is to develop, in the course of working with someone, an articulation of personal goals, purposes and values. It may also be useful to articulate with the person certain needs that are not fulfilled in his or her life.

Baumeister notes how research has not in fact supported the idea of Maslow's hierarchy of needs (1968), that is, the claim that we all move in the same way from safety to self-actualization. However, he does note that a particular individual might well have an idiosyncratic hierarchy of needs, that is, one unique to the person. Further, a personal hierarchy might change at different points in a person's life. It is this idiosyncratic system that needs to be explored.

The topic of motivation includes at least two quite different phenomena: one type is often described as desires, needs or wants, whereas another distinctive type of motivation is one of goals, aims,

23

plans and values. Some have argued that motivation in the form of goals is sometimes expressed in the form of a future narrative, for example, how someone might envisage a story of success at university followed by success at work. Kashima (1997) argues that a culture has typical stories and these stories suggest typical goals. Therapy can involve a new look at these unquestioned stories of how a person is supposed to live.

Loss and rediscovery of motivations

Several therapists have argued that many, if not all, forms of pathology involve a serious blockage and defeat of things the person needs and wants in life (Bowlby, 1969). The desires and needs of a person show themselves in many ways, and one way is in the sorts of narrations individuals repeat about their past and future. Wanting love, or a career, we imagine how this could develop: we daydream and fantasize, we tell ourselves and others stories of change and realization. We fear certain futures, but cannot stop ourselves imagining these worst-case scenarios.

In some forms of suffering there is perhaps an alteration or destruction of motivations. Needs are not satisfied and future goals are lost. Depression, I suspect, might well be in its essence a problem of destroyed person-constituting motivations (Rhodes and Smith, 2010) and as depression deepens, the loss of capacities such as being able to hope (Ratcliffe, 2010). In our research we noted how individuals had lost the most important and valued things in their lives, and now they felt utterly hopeless, that, in fact, 'life is over'. The influence of 'problem' and motive seems mutual and complex, and might be both consequence and cause.

However, it can also be said that for many psychopathologies, even simple phobias, the person is deeply demoralized and part of therapy must be to give the person some hope at least to attempt change.

The articulation of goals and values has always been central to the therapeutic practices of both de Shazer and White. Imagining a preferred future, tapping into lost hopes and needs, may be a key way to recruit the energy and the willpower to pursue change. Ratner et al. (2012), in their version of solution-focused therapy (SFT), place at the centre of their work the task of finding out about a person's 'hopes' for therapy, what that person hopes to have or change during therapy.

White (2007) has outlined many ways in which one can explore a person's direction in life and relevant values. If a client says that he or she wishes to have love or work, it is not just assumed that these are 'good', but instead White suggests we can explore why these are good for the client, what it is about getting a job that is good. By such questions the client can create a deeper articulation of why he or she wishes to move in that direction and in the process make his or her motivation for change stronger.

One of the strongest features of NSFT is that it not only encourages clients to think about problems and possible solutions, but sometimes asks them to step back and consider the general direction of their lives, to consider what they wish to live for.

6

Understanding behaviour

Intentional behaviours

I will assume, following the arguments of certain philosophers and psychologists, that everyday human action and interaction can be described as involving intentions to act and that the content of these intentions or decisions connects to a web of other 'intentional' features such as beliefs, desires and perceptions. Someone may be trying to make an everyday decision, for example, buy a printer. The person sees an advert, believes the object will do the tasks required and wants to print documents and photos. The person may then make a decision: 'OK, I'll buy this one'.

Conceptualizing human thought and action in these terms forms part of what philosophers called 'intentionality', in particular, that mental states are 'about' something, 'orientated' to something (Searle, 1983). There are many debates and differences of opinion concerning intentionality, but these are not relevant here. Some philosophers and many early behaviourists wished to get rid of all reference to and use of terms such as 'belief' or 'desire', but in contrast I will assume this is a useful way to talk of human action and perhaps one that is, in fact, utterly irreplaceable.

There are of course a multitude of other factors that do not at a particular moment enter a person's conscious thought at all: why is it the person trusts the website, the skills of typing the order, the history of debate concerning the need for a printer, and so on. Even a mundane decision to buy a printer has a context and history: understanding this history may be important for some problems, as we shall see next.

Analysis using the narrative frame

If we wish to understand in therapy a reported difficult episode in a person's life, or alternatively, to understand an often-repeated pattern of difficult behaviours, for example, not being assertive or getting angry, then a powerful framework for doing that is one of narrative, of telling a story or giving an account of what has happened in everyday language. This framework, I would suggest, is more useful in therapy than a classic behaviourist one of simple observable behaviours, of stimulus and response, and more useful than a cognitive one that assumes all behaviours are preceded by conscious and current thoughts.

The narrative analysis of behaviour is found in many areas of the humanities and in philosophy. The need for a narrative perspective is argued for by MacIntyre (1981), and how we can think of meaningful 'acts' and actions by Harré (1979).

The phenomenology of interaction

But what is 'behaviour' or 'interaction' really like? What does it involve? Ratcliffe (2007) cautions us against simplistic ideas. Reading some theories in psychology, one would assume interaction with another only involves thinking about the other person's thoughts, trying to work out that person's beliefs and desires. Ratcliffe, while accepting all those processes can occur, also underlines how interaction with others essentially involves bodily feelings, feelings in general, and understanding context. In addition, it involves a direct perceiving of meaning, emotions and the goals of others. Perhaps even more importantly, we experience another 'person', not an inanimate object or thing that we guess might be conscious. We are aware of the other as an agent, as a source of projects and possibilities: the other is someone who can influence how we ourselves act and feel, and that we too can influence.

We interact with others and show a whole series of 'expectations'. We may not be conscious of any such expectations, yet when the other does not react as in the past, and acts in ways that seem distinctly 'out of character' or out of role, we become aware of how what we expected has been challenged. Towards a person there may in fact be a sort of 'horizon' of expected possibilities.

To begin to articulate such non-verbalized expectations requires an attempt to narrate the history of how such reactions were learnt over time. According to the problem, person and therapy, one might trace this over a few years or even back to infancy.

A fundamental part of intimate relationships is trust: to close others we 'open' ourselves up, we trust they will behave in some ways and not others. Trust, however, is often lacking in those with serious difficulties, and we will return to this later.

Skills, habits and ways of behaving

There are a vast number of skills, habits and ways of doing everyday actions: we walk, cycle, talk in grammatically correct sentences, shake hands on greeting someone. We have skills and habitual ways of behaving at work and home. We also have habitual ways of being with other people: a person may be talkative or quiet, still or agitated, and so on.

When we watch different individuals, it is as if we see different 'styles' or personalities. In fact, it could be argued that individuals show their moods and character in each microsecond of their behaviour, in the very flow and style of the whole body, but also in the way the face moves, the eyes gaze, down to the smallest detail. Perhaps this is what Wittgenstein (1953) meant when he said the 'body' is the best picture of the 'soul'. I would qualify this by adding the living body, the body in process, is the best picture of the person.

We can form an intention to perform an action: for example, I decide to cycle to work, but the many skills I will then use (turning corners, braking, etc.) tend to emerge in a spontaneous flow. We tend only to become aware of these specific behaviours when a challenge occurs (for example, if the gears stop working).

There is therefore an important connection between our intentions (decision, beliefs and desires) and our habitual skilled behaviour flow, yet the two are not the same thing. We often cannot, for example, put into words how we carry out a complex motor skill such as change gears in a car. And certainly, perhaps only very skilled actors could begin to describe, or perform on demand, different styles of moving their body, of moving their face when laughing or when angry.

There are many theoretical discussions of the above issues. That many skills are learnt, yet cannot be put into explicit words, is an assumption of the theory of 'implicit' memory (Schacter, 1996). Neurological research suggests the brain may have different systems for motor patterns as opposed to parts that are crucial for forming intentions (Prinz, 2003). A great deal of evidence, reviewed by Bargh (2005), suggests that many behaviours, but also thoughts, can occur to a person 'automatically', that is, without conscious choice. For example, participants who read about old age in an experiment were recorded on a video as walking more slowly down the corridor in comparison to others who read about a different topic.

Of particular relevance to therapy is the fact that habitual behaviours are only partly under the conscious control of a person and some of these behaviours may be unpleasant or contributing to the suffering of a person. In a difficult social situation, habitual behaviours of 'withdraw' may manifest themselves, or the very opposite, habitual ways of making gestures or moving the body that signal aggression.

It may be that some high-speed habitual 'micro'-behaviours contribute to repetitive and destructive patterns of interaction. One client I worked with had a terror of others on the street. The first time I went out with him I was astonished to observe how he kept his head down, but when looking up, had a glare of intense aggression. He reported others being aggressive to him: I hypothesized that his 'way of being' on the street provoked fear or readiness for aggression in others. When discussed, he was completely unaware of the 'appearance', the 'emotional style' of his micro-behaviours. Direct observation of 'live' behaviours has always been emphasized both by systemic therapists as well as behaviourists and is part of NCBT.

Problematic patterns of interactions

It may well be that all psychopathologies involve, to some degree or other, significant ongoing repetitive problematic behaviours or interactions. That is, interactions, single or in sequences, that lead to immediate distress or which tend to reinforce a long-term difficulty. This seems to me to be true concerning depression and psychosis, but also for anxiety conditions. Possible exceptions might be very limited and specific problems, for example, a spider phobia, but of course, though such a person might have no obvious social difficulties, there are the specific behaviours of concern in the context of running away.

Sometimes problematic behaviour is something the client knows about and articulates as the central problem. For example, 'I get too upset in arguments'. However, sometimes the main presentation is of a feeling such as misery, or the state of being depressed, and if one asks about relationships, a multitude of problems are then articulated. The therapist may then hypothesize a connection.

That psychological problems are profoundly social, that they occur in a social context, is a fundamental assumption of all systemic therapies, including the work of de Shazer and White. This assumption is carried forward into NCBT.

Whether a specific social difficulty is a 'cause' of a state of depression, or a consequence, may be impossible to decide, and does not necessarily matter for doing therapy. In therapy the two are utterly intertwined, and one leads naturally to the other.

Many interactional problems can be thought of as having a relatively simple pattern or sequential structure. We might describe one pattern as follows: if x happens, then I do y, and later z. If someone is rude I clam up, but later curse myself and feel miserable. The person does not like doing y, in fact has carefully planned not to do it, yet once more it occurs. We may experience this as somehow out of our control: alternately, it might well be that we know we choose it but feel we just cannot resist it. The permutations, of course, are endless.

Whilst behaviour problems often seem to have a repetitive pattern, there is no reason at all to assume the person follows a conscious or unconscious 'rule' as such. Rather, the person has developed several dispositions which manifest themselves in context, just as our ability to cycle 'emerges' as we decide to get on a bike. We do not sit there trying to remember the 'rules' of balance. We decide to 'set off' as a deliberate intention and the actions flow. It might well be that many of our problems are a conflict between our dispositional self that is easily activated in the situation (to flee) and our conscious deliberate choice of goals (to stay put).

Whilst present difficulties may have emerged from a person's developmental history, it is also useful to remember that the present is continuously 'constructed', that a person brings a past but invents and improvises in the present world context, and in the context of an imagined future. The present is 'constrained', yet also open. Real interaction may appear to show aspects of a 'script', a pattern, yet is complex and essentially 'unknown' in the sense that we do not know how things will turn out, where a 'journey' will end.

I will not attempt to catalogue 'types' of interactive problems: if there are clear-cut types, then this is better studied in the context of specific pathologies, and lies outside this book. Further, to work with an individual, it often best to approach each person as unique and to attempt specific descriptions of idiosyncratic details.

Summary

To understand interactions, particularly ones seen as problematic, we need to explore both explicit intentions, but also their 'history', how they fit the wider aims, decisions and beliefs of a person. In trying to understand behaviour we also, however, often need to understand the 'texture' of a flow of spontaneous behaviours, the habits, skills and know-how, 'shown' in our actions. Both complex intentional actions and specific habitual behaviours can be relevant in therapy and both have a developmental history.

In thinking about complex interactions and behaviour we also need to remember that this is not just about simple bodily movements or even words, but the felt body, the flow of feelings, the perceptions of the other as agents together with subtle notions of expectation and trust, meaning and mutual influence, as described by phenomenologists such as Ratcliffe (2007).

Forming good intentions to change by clients in therapy is a first crucial step, but often not sufficient, particularly in the face of repetitive negative patterns. Here the person may need to learn new ways of being, or, which is perhaps easier, build on benign patterns that have been forgotten.

7

The network of meaning

It is sometimes useful in therapy to analyse in detail what has occurred during a difficult event for a patient. These events are the very sort that upset and disturb clients, for example, an intense feeling of fear or an unpleasant interaction followed by hours of disturbed emotion.

As a first step we might aim to document carefully 'what was happening'. A client described a situation at work where she felt 'told off' by her colleague. Here we can explore:

*   What did you feel?
*   What was the sequence of events?
*   What did you think? Did you have any images occurring?
*   And what did you do, think and feel afterwards?
*   Can you give a metaphor for how it felt?

The above can be complex and sometimes difficult: some clients seem to find it difficult to articulate feelings and upsetting events are remembered in a 'jumble', out of sequence, often with significant parts forgotten or not mentioned. In the end, however, the person has usually articulated a type of narrative.

Sometimes, if appropriate, we need to ask more:

*   Has this happened before with this person or others?
*   Do you always respond like this in these sorts of situation?
*   Why did you do, or not do, certain actions?
*   What was your role and the other person's role at this work place?
*   What did others say about it?

For this one event, there are therefore a very wide range of direct and indirect associated meanings, memories, ideas and ways of behaving. There are also several possible narratives, of recent similar events and ones from the past that could be explored if useful. Often if we ask about one detail, then it leads to other links, memories and ideas.

A person can be said to have a 'network' of associated beliefs, desires, ideas, narratives, metaphors, and so on. The concept of network derives from Searle (1983, 1992). His way of arguing for a network is as follows: if we take a statement such as, 'I want soup this lunch time, OK, I'll go to the shop', then there must be lots of linked beliefs and desires: for example, I believe there is a shop that sells soup not far from here; soup is tasty and I'm in the mood for it; the shop will be open today; I've got some money to buy it. For any event there will be some very closely linked beliefs/desires: however, as we follow the links, some are far removed yet are relevant: shops sell things I can buy, I am able to speak in English there, soup is healthy, and I want to stay healthy.

At any point in time, as we act, we are not thinking or feeling these things, yet might in certain conditions or situations: for example, I might discover the shop closed for a religious festival I was not aware of, might discover I have only a forged pound, etc.

Searle talks mainly of desires and beliefs in the network, but it is assumed that in any person's network, relevant to a topic, there are several potential states, feelings, assumptions and idiosyncratic links, and I would suggest many potential narratives. And in these narratives and ideas will be many metaphors, images and categories of the world.

Assessing network

Keeping in mind that a person has a unique personal network of meanings and intentional states reminds us that in trying to understand another person, we cannot assume 'words' always mean the same thing, or that others will 'construe' a topic in a similar fashion to ourselves.

I was struck by one depressed client telling me that the depressed are 'weak' and the 'weak' are 'ungrateful'. For me at first this was a quite baffling linking of ideas. I could only even begin to see how one could think like this after she explained her upbringing, giving a narrative of family ideologies and of claims made by her mother.

The term 'construe' here is explicitly borrowed from personal construct therapy (PCT) (Kelly, 1955; Winter and Viney, 2005). I think a great strength of PCT was that it emphasized that each person has a unique and idiosyncratic meaning system. Kelly suggested people have specific constructs, such as 'the weak are ungrateful', and that there will a sort of opposite 'pole' of meaning, e.g. 'the strong are …'. I believe that the idea of a personal network is an alternative to the version suggested by Kelly. The network concept can embrace various theories of meaning, and certainly has a place for narrative and metaphoric models.

In CBT a well-known technique has been that of 'downward arrow', where if someone makes a claim such as 'I have to make this job perfect' we might then ask, 'why must this job be done perfectly?' By repeated questions we then reach what may be 'core beliefs' such as 'I will only be respected if I do things perfectly' or 'If I am not respected, then I am worthless'. The technique of downward arrow assumes a network of meanings. I believe the concept of a network is in fact more flexible than the idea of a hierarchy of beliefs: there may or may not be core beliefs depending on the topic and person. The interconnection of meanings seems to spread in multiple 'dimensions' and many of these meanings are encapsulated in metaphoric models and episodic narrations.

8

The dispositional self

In the last chapter on network I argued there can be multiple narratives about a specific experience. A client had told me a narrative of being shouted at by a colleague at work. Yet around this specific narrative in the network were several other narratives, for example, times the other woman had shouted at her; how her colleague never 'listened'; how her mother had not listened in the past. All these layers of story are accessible by directly asking: to diverse extents, different clients can sometimes articulate relevant experiences.

The above, however, is not sufficient for understanding what happened. It is clear that the person in the situation acted in a specific way: stopped talking; walked away as soon as possible; displayed a type of expression on her face. Of course, there are things she did not do, for example, she did not shout back. Here the analysis is about complex actions and reactions: following Searle, it seems reasonable to think of these as either being manifest at the time in question or lying 'dormant', that at that time they were 'dispositions' and formed part of a person's repertoire of potential ways of interacting.

So, for a point in time, we might think of what is happening for a person as:

- manifest conscious experience of feelings, perceptions, thoughts, stories, ideas, actions and behaviours;
- a network of potential related ideas and narrations;
- a collection of behavioural dispositions and potential ways of reacting, perceiving and feeling.

Whilst at least in principle we can ask a person to tell us stories and beliefs, or how that person felt, it is difficult to access behavioural dispositions since they are the type of thing we 'do' or feel and not talk about. If a person can drive a car, he or she will be able to change gears: but our knowledge is 'procedural', it is not a set of verbal rules we can articulate. The same holds for a vast array of behaviours and for experience itself: the way we speak, our accent, our typical grammar, the way we move our body and our typical feelings and perceptions. These make up the behavioural-experiential repertoire of a person and, in fact, form a great deal of that person's identity.

The background

The concepts I am presenting here are very much influenced by Searle, and the notion of dispositions is a simplified and somewhat modified version of his concept of 'Background'. I do not want to develop fully the Background concept here since it is a complex philosophical notion. The concept is discussed in depth by Searle (1992). A colleague and I (Rhodes and Gipps, 2008) used it to illuminate how deluded patients lose background common-sense certainties, that is, things that may have just been taken for granted before their psychotic breakdown (for example, that others can be trusted, that walls are solid). The Background for a person is the total set of dispositions and capacities and abilities which allow the creation of any 'representation', any thought. The Background, however, is not itself made of representations or rules.

Some claims by Searle concerning the necessity of Background for meaning are controversial. The whole area of dispositions and what we take for granted has been discussed in diverse ways by several theorists (I shall not discuss these here). What is not controversial, however, and is very relevant to therapy, is that at any point in time most of our memories (of skills, habits), and most of our 'capacities' (such as a capacity for feeling fear or anger) are not activated. They are dormant and form a sort of 'repertoire' of potential behaviours and reactions. Furthermore, when activated, when 'unfolding', they are not the sort of thing we can easily put into words.

Bourdieu and the influence of culture

The concept of the self as dispositional is similar to that of 'habitus' in the sociology of Bourdieu (1990). He, like Searle, suggests that we do not learn conscious rules for social behaviours but, rather, 'absorb', 'pick up', how to act and react in specific ways. If we grow up in a culture, we acquire the ways of reacting 'typical' of that culture. For example, in different cultures there are typical distances people use when standing next to each other. The 'habitus' is that aspect of the person that 'generates' these typical ways of acting.

If we observe a group, we notice ways of behaving often different from our own, yet these ways seem 'natural' and 'obvious' to that group. Likewise, a 'family' can be said to have its own collective 'habitus' that manifests itself in ways of interacting and ways of taking things for granted.

The dispositional foundation of self

I wish now to pull together several of the ideas presented in the last few chapters, that is, of narrative, network, intentional behaviours and dispositional reactions.

We are not just made of stories and language, but are living embodied consciousness with a complex disposition to act in the world. In Figure 8.1, I outline a way experience can be conceptualized using the concepts of an accessible network of intentional states, but structured by the foundation of a dispositional self. The map describes a moment in time: a similar sort of map could be used to describe how a person develops over long periods of time.

The model presented here is meant both to underline the relevance of meaning, language and narrations, as well as how they coexist in the context of meaningful action or behaviour, and of living ongoing person-creating dispositions. The set of personal dispositions and network are products of our biology, history, culture and experience and are processes that create the unique individual.

41

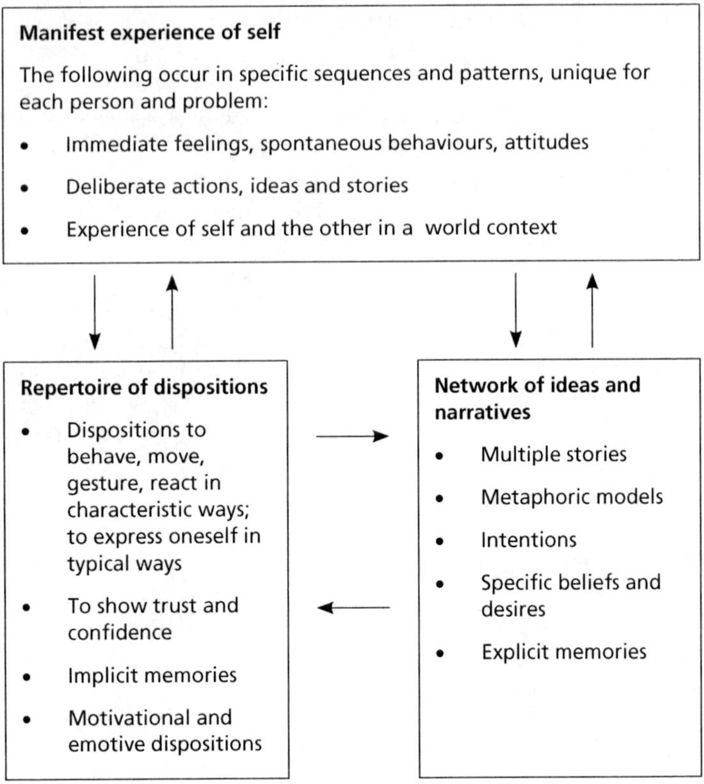

Figure 8.1 Map of the self in action.

Complex background dispositions are not 'rules' or 'beliefs'

Following Searle, I am not assuming the dispositions to behave are actually 'rules' or propositional beliefs. They are not 'theories', as Guidano and Liotti (1983) suggested. They are dispositions to act and react. Our personality is not therefore just a set of conscious beliefs; rather, it involves a skilled and complex way of behaving, a way of being and perceiving, developed over years in addition to whatever ideas and narratives the person holds.

A person is capable of very complex and diverse ways of acting: for example, the same person can be 'mature', yet at other times playful and irresponsible. We seem to absorb whole patterns and one person may have several quite separate patterns. Many branches of psychotherapy have pointed to this phenomenon: Young et al. (2003) talk of 'modes', and Ryle and Kerr (2002) use the concept of 'roles'. I wish to suggest that the concept of 'disposition', both simple and complex, might underlie these diverse models. When a person changes his or her global mood then perhaps a different set of dispositions and types of narrative are activated.

The unique person

The character of a person can be conceptualized in this narrative dispositional framework as follows. A person has an evolving narrative of self, of 'what I am', where from and where going, but in addition, the person has an evolving set of foundational dispositions that manifest themselves in diverse contexts. At any moment in time as we interact with a person, or observe him or her, we see or feel his or her personality-unique flow of behaviours and reactions. The person in the moment is that manifest flow of both narrative and emergent dispositions in the context of dormant narrations and a repertoire of potential dispositions.

For a person, his or her way of moving, responding and making gestures is 'taken for granted'. It is the way things are, or, rather, the way I am. These ways of being are acquired in a culture (Bourdieu, 1990) and the unique matrix of family experience, creating a personal 'habitus', the idiosyncratic way of being oneself.

In psychopathology, however, there is often a conflict or crash of narratives of self versus enacted dispositions: we wish to stop drinking alcohol, yet find ourselves just doing it. We wish to overcome our lack of confidence, but again we back off in fear. Our immediate reactions are not under our direct control. Fortunately, they are sometimes under indirect control, where we might, for example, try to induce a new feeling by putting ourselves in a new sort of situation. Another source of difficulty for a person is conflict between different narratives and between incompatible depositions.

Conclusion

Both normal experience and pathological experiences are complex processes unfolding over time. They involve explicit thoughts, feelings, actions and habitual behaviours. However, to understand why something does or does not occur, we might also need to examine relevant ideas, narrations and in-the-background ways of responding. Almost all these features will have a history.

The depth of understanding needed for therapy, however, is very variable. In long-term therapy, many of these aspects might be explored. In short-term therapy very little may be needed. The overall framework is, I believe, a useful map for whatever type of work we are doing.

9

The foundation of trust

Trust as a disposition

Normal social life could not function without trust. This ranges from the most intimate trust of close relationships to simple everyday trust that, for example, the postman really is a postman, and not a spy.

As we get to know a person better, we tend to trust him or her more and more. But how do we 'know' how to do this? Are there 'rules'? I think in fact there are no 'rules': rather, we have a 'know-how' – a way of developing trusting behaviours, perceptions and reactions. Our ability to trust, or not, is part of our foundational self-dispositions.

Moyal-Sharrock (2007), developing arguments of Wittgenstein (1969) and others, underlines the central importance of basic trust and certainty in the everyday world. We see a sort of trust in the youngest infant with its caretakers. Moyal-Sharrock notes how 'trust' cannot be understood as just a 'thought' or 'feeling': rather, it is a disposition, a way of being with others that manifests itself in diverse ways. In daily life with close others, we really do not normally think about this at all: we 'just do it', it forms part of our way of living. The concept of trust is precisely something I think we can make better sense of as an ongoing outflow of social dispositions to act and react in certain ways, in contrast to assuming a person has conceptual 'rules' or beliefs we can put into words.

Ratcliffe (2013) has also underlined the role of trust in interaction. Developing the argument made by Løgstrup, he suggests that intimate interaction involves being open to being influenced by the other, and that one in turn will affect the other: and thus we need to 'take care of the life which trust has placed in our hands' (Løgstrup, 1956).

Whilst I am highlighting trust here, I think very closely related topics are confidence and everyday certainties: they are sometimes different, yet often interconnected and sometimes interchangeable expressions. For example, I trust someone and am certain he or she will return some money or help out. Trust tends to be about people, but not always. Confidence tends to be about one's own activities, but it is also about others. Certainty is often about things and the world, but can be used for people too. There are perhaps also other related states, for example, having faith in oneself or others, or the evaluative attitude of saying 'I believe in you'.

When trust is broken

We just cannot live without certainty, trust and confidence. We cannot walk across the floor if we are not certain it is solid: we cannot pass strangers with ease if we feel they might attack, spit or condemn us. We struggle to go out to meet others if we have no confidence that we have something to say or that the others might not be interested. To live in a material and biological world, we need some everyday common-sense certainties, for example, that humans must eat food or that we should be careful crossing the road. In extreme psychosis, even certainties such as those seem suspended or lost (Rhodes and Gipps, 2008).

In clients, lack of confidence is so ubiquitous that, I suspect, we no longer see it. If we could do a survey of how many clients spontaneously mention it, I suspect the number would be very high indeed. I used to think when a client said he or she had lost confidence that it was just a different way of talking about anxiety: but I now believe it is something distinctive, and sometimes is more like a cause of anxiety than its consequence.

Traumas, developmental difficulties and severe challenges of adult years all unpick, suspend or undermine a person's certainties/trust/confidence. Herman (1992) underlined how loss of trust was a key feature of those who had experienced extreme trauma. I wish to suggest that any problem does not become a serious pathology unless certainty or trust is eroded to some degree. Lack of trust permeates pathology. It is a collapse of trust that undermines our capacity to begin to deal with a problem. And in order for therapy to work, then the client must rebuild trust and confidence: this cannot be done with reasoning or words alone.

Given there is a dispositional self of habitual behaviours and reactions, then erosion of trust/confidence might reflect changes at this very basic preverbal level. If so, this suggests that the growth of confidence is most likely to occur in a context of a trusting relationship to the therapist and one where the therapist shows trust/confidence in the capacity of the client to change, to take, for example, small, safe steps to doing that which is difficult. It may involve displaying to the client that one has confidence he or she can do a difficult task. Perhaps exposure therapies work not only because they alter fear itself, but because they encourage the acquisition and growth of confidence and trust in others, in the self and in the world.

10

Understanding the presentation of problems

In this chapter I will consider the presentation of symptoms and the client's perception of problematic contexts. There is a deep interconnection between the narratives a person holds and the events in his or her life. There is perhaps a sort of cycle whereby difficulties of living lead to the formation of narratives, but the latter in turn influence how a person lives. Some major types of experienced difficulties will be outlined.

Symptoms

There is a complex debate about the status of psychopathologies such as 'schizophrenia', but also depression and so forth. Whether we should think in terms of pathologies, if there are such things and whether our actual classifications are accurate, lies outside the scope of this book. I think different NCBT therapists would take diverse positions.

However, from the narrative perspective, I think this point is essential: we need to remember that each person's set of symptoms and problems is unique, and furthermore, that there can be unexpected and unique specific presentations. We need to be careful not to assume that if we describe someone as 'depressed', then we know automatically what that involves. Take any three clients who have sufficient in common to be described as 'depressed': it is still the case that each will have unique features and distinctive life histories. We should not be blinded by our conceptual 'filters', but, rather, we need to explore the unique pattern of suffering, of how this person experiences his or her life and situation, what he or she uniquely feels and does.

What is needed, I believe, is to explore the person's idiosyncratic narratives and his or her observed and reported patterns of living, and where possible to obtain 'near experience' (White, 2007) descriptions, in everyday language. Whatever causes symptoms, be it neurological change or symbolic meanings or something else, in the end it is manifest in phenomenology, in lived experience in a world. As therapists we need to keep that clearly in mind.

The relationship to others

Perhaps the most common topic of all in therapy is the relation between the self and close others: family, partner or friends. Sometimes these are the main problem: a client will talk of loneliness or conflict. But often, these areas are bound up in the person's experience of anxiety or depression. Qualitative research strongly points to disturbed relations and to disconnection in depression (Karp, 1996; Smith and Rhodes, in press).

Difficult relationships in childhood might be the major contribution to being vulnerable to events in adult years: that has always been assumed in most therapies, and CBT has always proposed that adult events can trigger schemas formed in childhood. I accept those ideas, yet also believe that it is possible that in some cases there are what may be thought of as person-destroying or person-wounding events during the client's adult years, that is, events so extreme that they change the person and create suffering where there had been no predisposing developmental vulnerability. Examples of being transformed are found after major trauma and/or loss.

Following great difficulties or trauma, in early life or adult years, the model here presumes that this will leave traces in both narrations of the self and in depositional reactions, in the repertoire of behaviours and felt experiences.

Experiencing society

We live in a 'society' and this influences a person in many ways. One route of influence is through collective representations, that is, 'pictures' and 'stories' that circulate in the media and in discourse. Many of these collective pictures and stories can be oppressive, particularly for any group which finds itself to be in a minority position. There are also stereotypes of 'male' and 'female' and a person can feel oppressed, and in fact, be oppressed, if he or she finds that he or she does not fit these rigid images. Wilkinson and Pickett (2009) argue that a key mechanism is the influence of society on a person's self-esteem.

Society also influences individuals through the events of history, such as war and conflict. In London, many clients are refugees fleeing war or oppression. To understand such patients we often need not only to pay attention to immediate symptoms of, for example, depression or 'voices', but the wider experience of being exiles and experiencing an 'alien' society. Clients struggle to make sense of the extraordinary events that have occurred to them (Parrett et al., 2013).

A major problem for many clients is that they cannot work: the problems this can cause are many, but certainly one aspect is that clients often feel a kind of 'shame' about this, that they are outside normal society. One group of clients I worked with clearly articulated this to me in a discussion concerning shame. These themes are strong for those who suffer chronic psychiatric conditions such as psychosis. Such clients report feeling they have no 'place' in society, that they are of 'no use'.

The sense of existence

We each experience time, change and loss: we might or might not have a sense of purpose, meaning, or value and that our lives have some sort of direction. Many philosophers and therapists have written about this (Cooper, 2003).

The unease or 'gap' a person might feel is often not brought at first to therapy but can emerge later: in contrast, such topics can be very conspicuous for those who suffer severe displacement in their lives, for example a refugee who loses family and a whole career.

Conclusion

There are a multitude of possible presenting problems and sometimes it is therapeutic in itself to explore these, and perhaps only attempt much later some sort of problem solving and/or solution finding, if appropriate, with the client. However, whether it is wise to do that depends on the attitude of the client. For some, any further exploration of difficulties is unwelcome and in such cases it is better not to proceed with examining difficulties. Better then to focus on ways forward. Some clients, however, clearly state that they do wish to explore painful difficulties both of present times and the past, and report that they find this therapeutic. It is true that often there are distortions or statements made by clients that allow no hope for change, but from my observation I note that many clients have suffered a range of real difficulties and these continue to place them in challenging situations. We need to remember there is a 'world', that problems are not just about interpretation.

11

How does therapy create change?

How does therapy work? If a person stops being depressed during therapeutic treatment, what actually changes in or about the person? What aspects of therapy have caused or influenced this change? Brewin (2006) reviews some standard theories given in CBT.

One classic argument is as follows: part of being depressed is having terrible negative cognitions such as 'I'm an utter failure' or 'the future can only be one of more suffering'. In CBT these beliefs are questioned: ideally the therapist encourages the person to question these by asking the person to look for inconsistencies, overgeneralizations, evidence that does not fit or contradicts the negative thoughts and beliefs, the latter sometimes being called cognitive structures or content.

Brewin, however, critiques this theory. During a course of CBT a person can stop being depressed, but a few months or years later can become depressed again. Often the same sort of negative thoughts recur for that person. If the cognitive content had been really changed, why has it returned?

A similar argument is made against classic behavioural explanations of change, for example, in work with phobias. A person can undergo exposure therapy and begin to go out to public places, but under stress the same fear returns. If exposure therapy really does change some sort of fear 'connection' or 'structure', whether in the mind or brain, why has the fear returned? How is that possible? Brewin points out that there is considerable evidence that certain types of fear or intense emotional memories seem long-lasting, if not permanent.

Reviewing such evidence and other research, Brewin proposes a different explanation for change. When someone changes, the most important thing might not be that the negative content has been permanently altered, or erased in some sense, but rather that the person develops new positive ideas, beliefs and associations about how to cope or positive beliefs about himself or herself. A person may move from always thinking 'nothing I do works' to 'sometimes things go well' or 'I can cope with this setback and can try again'.

Therapy might help clients change in such a way that they can experience a retrieval of positive meanings or 'representations' in the relevant difficult situation. Furthermore, therapy can work to make these new benign meanings more distinctive, well rehearsed and significant to the person.

Of relevance to this book is the fact that Brewin speculates on whether his explanation might apply to other therapies, however different from each other these therapies might seem on first inspection. He explicitly mentions White and Epston's narrative therapy (1990), in particular that the building of a new narration of the self is a very clear example of building a new complex set of positive representations. Making these links to other therapies also connects to an earlier argument of Brewin and Power (1999), that there may be common mechanisms in different therapies and that one of these is about changing meaning.

It is clear that one of the central purposes of narrative therapy is to build a whole network of new meanings, new stories of the self. The same, however, also holds for de Shazer's solution-focused therapy where a central idea is to generate ideas of 'what works', and what the client could try to do more of. In Brewin's terms, the solution-focused idea of 'exceptions', that is, times things have gone well, might lead to new positive representations or thoughts, such as, 'Yes, I was brave last time I went on the bus, so perhaps I could do what I did last time to see if it works'.

Brewin talks of 'representations', and certainly these may occur in the form of ideas, images, or narratives for a person. However, NCBT assumes that psychological experience involves more than just 'representations'. Feelings in the body or states of relaxation cannot be conceptualized in terms of representations only. Instead of only talking of 'representations', it may be that we also need to talk of potential dispositions. In these terms then therapy might be said to have worked if it creates access to positive ideas (perhaps in the network), but in addition, if it creates, or leads to the rediscovery of, benign dispositions which can be activated in the problematic situation. Some of these dispositions will create conscious skills and habits, while more subtle dispositions might create preverbal feelings or a new experience of trust and confidence. Some of these dispositions might be created but of which we have no direct awareness; we just feel different, feel 'confident'. That is, they are 'activated' and influence our conscious experience, but remain at a background level.

How to make ideas memorable?

Brewin argues that representations need to be distinctive and well practised, and should be of significance to the person. One way of being very distinctive is to express ideas, negative and positive, in the form of metaphors or narratives. Putting any changes that a person makes into the context of a new story of self provides a sort of 'frame', and thus makes these changes more vivid and easy to remember.

Being positive about what?

The arguments of Brewin, I believe, are illuminating. However, it also seems reasonable to suggest that building coping skills and positive ideas is easier with a client if there are in fact things the person can be positive about in his or her world. One of the great strengths of behavioural activation (Martell et al., 2001) is that it helps individuals to make changes in their world, to solve real problems that matter to them and to face up to tasks they are avoiding yet which they know are really important for them.

MacLeod and Moore (2000) have argued that personal 'resources', that is, any good and constructive things, from friendships to hobbies, can act as 'buffers' against the experience of negative events. One aim of NCBT (Rhodes and Jakes, 2009) is in fact

55

to help individuals not only build benign representations, but where possible, to help them make changes in their life or environment and to seek good things in the world. At the very simplest level this is not necessarily about making complete changes but about appreciation of daily good things available to almost everyone, such as a walk in the park, or really listening to a piece of music. Other ideas for enriching the person's environment are encouragement to engage in any type of community group or to learn new hobbies.

In sum, one theory of therapy suggests that change may occur by finding positive and distinctive ideas of self that are remembered by the person with ease and are of personal significance. Changing the actual environment of the person may help this process. There are of course many other aspects that can help to make therapy work, such as the therapeutic relationship, compassion and the building of trust. We will discuss some of these in coming sections.

12

How narrative might help

The theory of Brewin emphasized what may occur when therapy is successful, that is, a new access to positive representations in relevant difficult situations. Cozolino (2010) also writes about the process of therapy, emphasizing common processes that might occur in all types of therapy, and, in particular, how these might relate to changes in the brain.

Cozolino argues that he has identified from the literature four processes that evidence suggests lead to the healthy development of the young brain, and that these same four processes are encouraged by carrying out therapeutic work. The four are:

1. Being put in a situation of 'optional stress', or perhaps, it might be clearer to say, optional challenge: for example, a person is encouraged to do a feared and difficult thing. Evidence suggests that brains become more complex in rich environments.
2. To be placed in a warm, caring relationship. This of course is the extremely well-known area of therapeutic 'alliance', or working relationship, the sort of area articulated as essential by Rogers (1951), and certainly overlapping with compassion (Gilbert, 2010). I will return to this in another chapter.
3. To be encouraged to put together – to interconnect – thought with emotion and emotion with thought. Siegle (1999) suggested that the left and verbal side of the brain needs to work with the right side, the latter containing autobiographic memories. Gerhardt (2004) notes how the developing child brings together many systems of the brain, and that with the emergence of language, neural connections are formed between left and right brain. Clearly a central role of cognitive therapy has always been to think and reflect on feelings with clients: how

did a feeling start? What beliefs are relevant? In most narrative therapies, and in the emotion-focused constructivist therapy of Greenberg (2002), a central task is to find words for feeling and sensations.

4. Developing a narrative is also seen as essential. From a neurological point of view, it is suggested that the act of developing narrative encourages connections of left to right brain, but also top-down, that is, the development of connections from the higher cortex to areas of emotion generation deep in the lower parts of the brain such as the amygdala. The person can then move from a jumble of impressions to a coherent and manageable story.

To give further details is outside the scope of this book, yet it is fascinating to note that many books linking therapy, the brain and development, often mention the profound and crucial role of narrative, of our ability to generate autobiographic accounts.

I wish to suggest that NCBT incorporates all four processes outlined by Cozolino: the articulation of narrative; the encouragement of clients to perform new and difficult tasks; thinking and expressing emotions about avoided topics; and the formation of a warm and constructive therapeutic relationship.

Encouraging clients to put their feelings and experiences into metaphors is also an example of how one can bring cognition and emotion together. Asking a person to construct a metaphor for how he or she felt during a difficult episode is precisely to think and verbalize with and about one's feelings.

Following the argument of Ratcliffe (2007), I think it is interesting to relate phenomenology to the working of the brain given that this is not an attempt to get rid of either side of the equation. That therapy on the one level changes conscious felt experience, but simultaneously on another level is an alteration in the brain, to me seems feasible and informative. The research evidence is minimal and speculation extreme, yet such scientific integration seems wise and may help us to identify key processes and needed directions in our work.

Other ideas on narrative and change

Another line of research has been carried out by Pennebaker (1990). His research suggested that it helps clients with many problems if they express their difficulties in writing. The benefits seem to be very wide-ranging and include actual improved physical health for some, in addition to improvements in mental health. He speculates that 'repression', the not expressing of something which is of concern, is a process that uses up a lot of energy, and that expression changes this.

Neuner and colleagues (2002), who developed a therapy for refugees which involves the putting of traumatic memories into narrative, have researched their work and found positive results in terms of changes in symptoms. In one experiment the same researchers (Adenauer et al., 2011) examined the brains of patients before and after treatment and claim results indicated lasting changes in specific areas concerning vision and attention.

So far I have discussed changes on a psychological level and a neurological one: I suspect, however, that there are many other changes. Some anthropological research suggested that telling a story of trauma in culturally prescribed ways, in the presence of a group, was the way that American indigenous Indians survived the effects of being in the Vietnam war (O'Nell, 1999). Perhaps telling a story to others somehow changes our role in a society.

In sum, there is now emerging evidence that the act of narration, in particular of one's suffering, can have a benign effect on a wide range of aspects of the person and his or her experiences, yet may also involve long-term changes in the connections and functioning of the brain.

13

Learning from the client and building trust

Bliss and Bray (2009) attempt, and I think succeed, in giving a minimal definition of when therapy is solution-focused. They note how many writers have tried to identify a defining set of techniques, for example, a focus on exceptions or the use of future-focused questions. Yet these lists of techniques tend to differ.

Their resolution is to focus on the relationship between the client and therapist, and suggest that what makes therapy uniquely solution-focused is the 'co-construction aspect that requires that the therapist learn from the client'. To learn from the client here means that, in the search for a solution, the therapist might ask what has worked, or might explore how the client imagines the future. Then, with the client, the therapist thinks and builds up a suggestion for change using the ideas and words of the client.

CBT does not work like this: usually the problem is analysed using a standard set of concepts, for example, 'negative cognitions', and the problem is explained using these concepts, and then a typical technique is suggested. The technique is meant to match the problem: if there are negative thoughts, then these should be challenged. I do think this standard approach can be useful sometimes, and NCBT uses 'challenging' in some contexts, but it is definitely not the approach of solution-orientated therapies.

After their first definition, Bliss and Bray then move on to the wider picture: they agree with the idea that SFT involves curiosity and respect, and being tentative. The therapist asks questions he or she does not know the answers to, and listens to the answers with a constructive ear. Most typically, but not essentially, the following might be observed:

1. Asking about a preferred future;
2. Exploring how both will know they are moving in the right direction;
3. Finding out what the client can do more of, or do differently, to start moving in that direction;
4. How the client will know he or she has done enough therapy.

They suggest no time frame, hence therapy could be 'brief' or extended in time, and still solution-focused.

Can this be combined with the use of CBT?

A pure SFT would use the above and only the above. For many clients and problem presentations, I think that is the most useful and practical way forward, for example, in chaotic situations, or where it is sure there may only be a couple of meetings, or where clients are clearly 'ambivalent' about seeing someone.

Given that the essence of an SF approach is this attitude of building client-generated solutions, then it seems possible that this attitude is compatible with other therapies and in particular with techniques from CBT. This integration or fusion is achievable in several ways, to different degrees.

In general, one would first prioritize the very solutions generated by clients, but later, if necessary, there could also be a sharing of relevant knowledge. The stance of the therapist here would be: other people with similar problems, for example, fear, have found this useful. Would you like to try this method? How could you modify it for your context and purpose?

One can introduce techniques, but also explanatory concepts: for example, many patients have not heard of 'rumination' but quickly recognize it when described as part of depression. Use of this sort of knowledge is, of course, a kind of 'expertise', but it is not an expertise of saying: I fully understand you and your problem, and here is the scientific answer.

Building trust

The solution-focused attitude of learning from the client relates directly to trusting and having confidence in clients, and asking them to begin to trust themselves.

As stated earlier, the erosion of certainty/trust/confidence is a key change in diverse psychopathologies. When clients arrive in therapy, they often feel demoralized; they have a problem, and attack themselves for not being 'strong' or 'clever' enough to be able to solve the problem. They have a problem, and are distressed by the fact of having a problem: by this time clients have often 'given up'. The attitude of solution focus goes against that: it is one of, 'let's see if together we can discover something, or make something that works. Let's see what you bring to the table and may just have forgotten or not seen. Perhaps you have abilities you have overlooked, abilities which are just switched off at the moment.'

It is not, however, just about finding easy things that already work. Sometimes the position is more like the following: we need to do something very difficult, we need to build a coherent narrative of painful memories in order to move forward, and I believe you have the capacity, I notice in fact how you did manage in the past.

14

The theory of problem patterns, exceptions and goals

In this chapter I want to present some ideas about problem patterns, drawing on SFT and systemic therapy in general. Many solution-focused therapists have rejected theories of pathology and therapeutic mechanisms, but following Lipchik (2002), I think there is a need for theory and will sketch some ideas.

In the field of SFT, de Shazer (1985, 1988) carried out what seems to me a sort of 'action research' or applied multi-case study, that is, they observed their own practice and attempted to identify 'what worked'. They applied these techniques to further cases and types of presentation in cycles of reflection and practice. They did not therefore base their therapy on an explicit theory of change.

Lipchik was a member of this early team: she believes the above process generated many new therapeutic ideas, but warned that in the years since there had developed an overemphasis on pure technique. She advocated the return to theory and a return to basic therapeutic issues such as awareness of emotion, therapeutic relationships and the articulation with the client of what the problems actually are. That is, there certainly are clients who cannot put into words what their problems or goals might be and for such clients we do need to explore their experience of difficulties. I agree with Lipchik on these points and also agree that research in diverse areas, including neuropsychology and emotions, is useful.

Key topics of exploration in SFT are exceptions to a problem and goals and hopes. I will discuss these in turn.

Exceptions and negative interactive patterns

In the earlier work by de Shazer (1985), he was influenced by the central idea of 'strategic' family therapy, that all problems occurred in families due to repeated negative patterns. For example: a child wets the bed, and then the parents shout and blame the child. This occurs again and again. There are more complex patterns and different families have unique patterns. In some, a pattern may be: the child wets the bed; the couple argues about parenting style; the grandmother comforts the child.

An essential insight of SF therapists was, however, that no problem pattern is 'perfect'. It may be reported as 'exactly the same', again and again, yet it just turns out to be the case that real-world patterns are messy and chaotic, and that change at some level (from micro-behaviours to attitudes) is occurring, be it slowly or in sudden stages.

When there are exceptions it may be the case that something has occurred that influenced the pattern, has had in fact some causal effect. Alternatively, it might be the case that the very same family can follow two very distinctive interactive patterns, one involving 'wet beds' and one with contented sleep and a dry bed. In spite of having these 'capacities', the family does not know how to switch from one to the other.

The concept of repetitive patterns, it seems to me, is still a useful concept if it is taken as occurring at least for some pathologies (not necessarily for all), and assuming that other levels of explanation are in fact relevant.

I wish to hypothesize that the concept of negative patterns makes sense in terms of the concepts used in earlier chapters. If there is a repetitive pattern between persons A and B, then a pattern might become routine because the two persons are repeatedly activating dispositional 'habits' in each other. For example: person A does not answer a question; this triggers a 'mistrust' attitude in B who then retaliates with criticism, to which A responds with further evasive behaviour.

But other patterns could emerge, precisely because each person is complex and has many 'sides': person B might be in an extra good mood, so instead of retaliating, just cracks a joke. And why was he in a good mood? Well, he often is just after going to the gym.

The search for exceptions can discover behaviours, habits, in fact practically anything, which could be 'highlighted' and then used deliberately to generate solution patterns. The negative is replaced by something new. It may be that solution-orientated dispositions had been in the 'background', or dormant, and now become foreground, centre stage. The dialogue concerning exceptions leads to a new narrative of the problem/solution, but also is part of the attempt to change behaviour and dispositions in context.

Goals

I do not think in the psychological literature there is as yet one comprehensive theory of why knowing one's goals may help change. There are, however, many partial theories and clues.

An absolutely central part of SFT has been the construction in words and images of future goals, of working with a person to articulate 'hopes' (Ratner et al., 2012). De Shazer himself quotes long-established findings that goals are helpful if clear, doable and given as small steps.

More recent research has talked of 'implementation intentions' (Gollwitzer et al., 2005). That is, in experimental conditions, participants who have articulated not only 'goals' ('take up the gym'), but how they are going to implement this intention, when and what steps will be taken, are more likely to make changes. Gollwitzer et al. suggest that this might be in part that such articulation recruits processes of 'automaticity', that is, in the relevant situations certain goals will be unconsciously activated.

SF therapists ask not only about the 'future' goals of a person, but how something has been done or could be done. When a 'success' is reported, questions such as 'how did you manage to do that?' and 'how did you prepare yourself?' are used. These all encourage 'implementation intentions'.

Conclusion

SFT innovated practical ideas in the areas of repetitive personal and interpersonal patterns, of naturally occurring 'exceptions' and of goal construction. I see no reason for not integrating such approaches within a science of psychotherapy and CBT.

The negative pattern is, I suspect, held in place by many forces. One certainly is the use of negative fixed narrations by clients. Another, as argued, is the existence of various types of disposition, of entrenched behavioural, emotive and attitudinal states of the person, with all these occurring in the wider material and symbolic context of a person's daily life. Yet within the network of many narratives and the multitude of dispositional states, sometimes benign areas can be found and solutions generated.

15

Integrating theory and practice

Overview

Putting the themes of the chapters on therapeutic change together underlines the central importance of several processes, in particular:

- The need to articulate a narrative of problems and sometimes for a person to be helped to find the actual words;
- The need to construct new benign narratives and find ways of coping, of changing, and doing something new, to build new things in a person's real life and world. Given negative patterns might not go away but only lie dormant, the person needs alternatives in order to cope with or circumvent difficulties;
- A person needs to learn ways of not triggering negative dispositional patterns, but either to build, or better yet, to recruit present benign dispositional patterns. The person needs to learn to trust and have confidence in these ways of doing;
- Therapy is facilitated if we trust the person to generate ideas, to use his or her 'constructs', categories and ways of talking. Interventions make most sense when generated by the person's own creative processes;
- Sometimes, however, clients do not provide information that leads to change, and then, however difficult, it might be best to see how ready-made interventions can be tailored for the specific person.

Pathology

The chapters on key features of the self and pathology point not only to the importance of negative and destructive narratives, but also to the key importance of the outflow of foundational dispositions in terms of ways of behaving, feeling and trusting.

Many people in the grip of suffering find themselves locked in a 'problem-saturated story', but they also find themselves locked in the grip of interactive negative patterns, and often the 'story' and the way of being only act to reinforce each other. There is a sort of downward spiral of negativity, and at each turn, there is less positive motivation to live and declining trust and confidence. People lose their sense of purpose and value.

Furthermore, these periods of suffering occur in a real-world context of resources, challenges and meaning. Often these have become impoverished or destroyed. A great deal of pathology, I believe, is a response to or perception of the real world. Of course, there can be 'distortions' and 'blindness' to positive areas, yet I cannot think of a patient who is not either responding to recent problems or alternatively is experiencing consequences created by a difficult childhood.

Specific pathologies might require specific ways of carrying out therapy and assessment. In Part 2 I will give some outlines on how there may be adaptations for depression, trauma, obsessive-compulsive disorder and refugees.

Who is NCBT suitable for?

We can think of client presentations as forming three very approximate 'types':

1. Specific presentations: well-defined problems such as phobia.
2. Complex presentations: there may be several symptoms at once, or serious issues from the past. This would include psychotic presentations, chronic depression and problems of 'comorbidity'.
3. Extreme problems of instability; extreme and chronic emotional difficulties.

I would suggest that basic CBT or NCBT are useful for the first type: NCBT is particularly useful if there are issues of the past.

I think NCBT is very suitable for complex presentations. Working with extreme instability and personality disorders in general requires very long-term work, often with an extended focus on the therapeutic alliance. One such approach is that of schema therapy (Young et al., 2003).

Research on effectiveness

Research suggests SFT itself has outcomes comparable to other therapies (see Gingerich and Eisengart, 2000, for a review). One trial has looked specifically at a narrative approach for depression and found good outcomes (Vromans and Schweitzer, 2011).

A colleague and I presented data to suggest that a solution-focused phase had an effect upon social difficulties (Jakes et al., 1999) and on delusions (Jakes and Rhodes, 2003). O'Connor and associates have carried out extensive assessment of their approach (see Chapter 30). There are considerable outcome data for narrative exposure therapy and traumas (Neuner et al., 2002).

Whether NCBT is comparable or not to other therapies in general trials, I do wish to suggest that the approach of NCBT offers a flexible, creative and practical approach that allows adaptations to the complexity of individuals.

Part 2

THE DISTINCTIVE
PRACTICAL FEATURES
OF NARRATIVE CBT

16

First encounters and therapy planning

A first task in meeting a patient is to ascertain what the patient is seeking or in fact not seeking. Only last week I met a patient for the first time who quickly told me that she had not asked for therapy and did not want it. Solution-focused therapy and other systemic approaches have always shown sensitivity concerning this topic: in schools or hospitals, for example, it is not rare for someone to think therapy might be a 'good idea' for someone else and then use over-enthusiastic persuasion or even send the individual, without asking, to a therapist.

Several sorts of questions can help clarify the above, and more generally, what goals the client is seeking. For example:

* Whose idea was it to seek therapy?
* What do you hope may happen by coming to therapy?
* What would you like to aim for?
* What other therapies or activities have you tried?
* Given what has happened, do you really wish to attend? Is that OK with you?

Sometimes it is then useful, where there is obvious doubt, to suggest to the client that he or she thinks it over and makes contact with the therapist if and when ready.

Basic assessment

Given the client is interested in therapy, then other areas to explore in the first interview might be:

- How does the client perceive his or her problems at present?
- Who is in the client's world?
- What is the client's home, work, or education situation?
- To enquire about other symptoms;
- To give questionnaires concerning levels of anxiety or depression;
- To give appropriate tests for specific symptoms such as voices, obsessive-compulsive disorder, posttraumatic stress disorder, etc.;
- A brief outline of childhood and early years.

It is useful to see the first session, or part of the session, as a sort of intake and planning meeting. It is a highly focused assessment to decide later what might need exploring in more depth, and what sort of approach would be suitable. In the service I work for, we make this initial assessment and then discuss with the client potential ways forward. In some cases it can be better to refer on to a more appropriate service. Care and attention are particularly required with psychotic clients or with those clients who present with either alcoholic or suicidal behaviour.

Therapy planning

In NCBT one major decision is whether to offer:

1. Immediate solution-orientated work for the presenting difficulties, or
2. More extended and full NCBT where there is further indepth narrative exploration of difficulties before moving on to therapeutic interventions.

Using 'pure' solution-focused work is extremely useful in situations where, for whatever reason, there is little time, or some action is required by an urgent difficulty. See Chapter 20 for further details.

If a client presents with a problem suitable for therapy, such as depression, interpersonal difficulties or voices, and furthermore seems motivated to attend and to seek help, then it can be useful to design a therapy plan and share this with the client.

Different presenting difficulties and different personalities require different therapy plans or 'pathways'. One sequence I have used many times for delusions and voices (Rhodes and Jakes, 2009) unfolds as follows:

- The initial assessment concerning attitude to therapy, that is, whether there is a motivation for engaging in change and attending;
- A narrative of the presenting symptom and/or presented problems, while also giving attention to the establishment of alliance;
- Solution-focused work or any work aimed at coping in the present, sometimes using additional CBT techniques such as behavioural activation, emotion regulation skills, exposure or relaxation training where appropriate;
- Therapy exploring core beliefs about self and others with the aim of constructing a conception of a preferred self. Where appropriate there is a focus on developing compassion for self;
- If considered useful by the therapist, and most of all the client, a narrative exploration of past difficulties and trauma but also helping to construct a narrative of past strengths and resources, and examples of when the person lived in a preferred way;
- If symptoms such as voices or delusions are still having an impact on daily life, then investigating alternative narratives and beliefs about delusions and voices and locating triggers for symptoms;
- A phase exploring building resources, changing the environment, and increased involvement in the community and finally the process of leaving regular therapy.

Chapter 29 outlines a specific pathway for working with depression.

The art of being flexible

An essential point in beginning to work with clients is that we must really try to see both the problems from the point of view of the client as well as understand the client's attitude to the problem and how it should be solved. We should not assume a standard way of assessing and way of proceeding in therapy that must be followed. We need to remain open and flexible.

17

Constructive narration of difficulties

There are several ways of using narrative to explore specific problems and symptoms, but of course narrative can also be used to explore a person's whole life. The work described here is envisaged as usually taking place in the early phase of therapy where it has been agreed that a focus is first needed on the presenting problems. One might return to these if new problems, or a new focus, emerge in the course of the work.

A simple but useful map is to think of:

- Narratives focused on problems, challenges, difficulties in living;
- Narratives that suggest ways forward; areas where life has gone well; ideas for how to live in the future.

This chapter focuses on the first.

For many problem presentations a relatively small number of sessions for exploration are usually sufficient. For severe trauma some clients require far more work; trauma is covered in Chapter 22.

It helps to think of the general movement of therapy as being from problem to solution, but there is often an oscillation between the two when, en route, new aspects are revealed and there is a need for further problem narration.

While the following approaches to problems will be described separately in this chapter, in practice they can be combined in various ways.

Basic narrative exploration of the present

First it is useful to explore ongoing problems as they occur in the present.

- Tell me about your present difficulties. How do you see your difficulties at present?
- You mentioned you are feeling depressed, what is that like? What do you experience on a daily basis?

The client can be asked to narrate examples of problems that have very recently occurred, and sometimes asked to keep a weekly record of relevant events. These might be thought of as micro-narrations. One written task can be:

- We have discussed x (your family arguments). If one occurs this week, please write in detail the sequence of what occurred. Note your feelings, thoughts and reactions. Think if there is a metaphor for expressing how you feel.

At this stage any method of assessment such as standard questionnaires for depression or anxiety can be added if useful.

A narrative of past events

For many presentations, exploring the onset of difficulties and their meaning is highly informative, for example, the onset of extreme anxiety:

- When did this start?
- What was going on in your life before?
- When these things began to happen, what did it mean to you?
- What happened next? And how did this develop?
- How did it influence other areas of your life?
- How did you feel when these things occurred?
- How did this influence the way you saw yourself?

Exploring the history of difficulties can be a therapeutic piece of work in itself. Many clients have never expressed what has happened to them. The work of finding words for meaning and feelings, of

CONSTRUCTIVE NARRATION OF DIFFICULTIES

putting events in context, of reflecting on what this path of development might mean, all seem beneficial.

Constructional narrative exploration

White and Epston (1990, 2007) innovated many approaches that not only allow clients to explore the history of problems, but at the same time gently open up the possibility of moving on to solutions and change. The following sequence of questions is particularly useful.

Naming the problem

The client is invited to step back and think of a description or a name for the problem.

• If you were to name this problem, what would you call it?
• What is your typical way of describing this difficulty?

White and Epston suggest the description should be 'near-experience', that is, one capturing the experience of the client in his or her own everyday words. CBT, I believe, can learn a great deal from narrative therapy on how to give attention to the actual words used by clients, and on the attempt to construct idiosyncratic descriptions that are expressive for the client.

Effects of the problem

Problems do not exist in isolation: they influence and are influenced by practically anything in the person's world.

• What influence has this problem had on your life? For example, your relationships, views of self, or way of living?

Effects are often 'systemic', for example, a phobia about dogs could lead to a couple having arguments about walking in the park.

The presence of a 'voice' can make a person feel self-conscious since he or she believes its manifestation might somehow be seen by others, and in turn, this leads to withdrawal. Whilst it might seem very 'negative' to unearth yet more difficulties, these associated areas can be later explored for solutions.

Evaluating the problem and its effects

I think a wise practice of narrative approaches has always been not to assume an apparently negative thing is in fact negative for a person, nor to assume, if reported negative, the reason why it is negative. My reason for thinking something like depression is terrible may not be the client's reason.

- You have described voices as shouting at you. Are these voices things you wish to have or not have in your life? What is negative about them? What is it that you do not like? Is anything positive?

Justifying the evaluations

Given something is experienced as negative, the client can be asked to articulate his or her reasons for this:

- You said the depression stops you socializing and you do not like that. Why is that? Why is that not OK for you?
- What does this tell you about what you want and do not want for your life?

Such questions can reveal the values and aspirations a client holds (see Chapter 24 for an example).

Personification

A variation on the above involves asking the client to describe a problem as a 'character' and as 'external' to the person.

- How does depression stop you from meeting others? How does it put you down?
- How do the voices find ways of intimidating you? What tricks have they played?
- How does this habit sneak up on you and persuade you to follow its path?

To form such questions, ideally one uses words (such as 'tricked') already said by the client. From clinical observation this seems to be something clearly liked by some patients. Perhaps it somehow involves our imagination. The constructional advantage is that later one can ask how to develop different and new relations to the voices or depressions using these personifications.

Network analysis

As discussed in Chapter 7, we sometimes need to explore not only explicit statements, but how these ideas link to others not expressed, and yet which may have a role. Some ways we can begin to find out about a person's network are as follows.

- Ask for relevant narratives or metaphors about a problem, then explore the implications of the metaphor.
- Focus on feelings and ask for descriptions, then consider where these lead.
- Ask 'why' questions and 'if …, then …'; for example, 'if you did speak up, what would happen?'
- Sometimes one can use imagery: for example, ask the person to imagine the problem as it happens and articulate what is happening.
- The client can be asked to role-play and therefore 'show' the relevant behaviour.
- Typical cognitive therapy questions such as 'downward arrow' can be used (see Chapter 7).
- Use modified personal construct questions, such as 'you say your friend is "bossy", but how would you describe someone who is the very opposite of "bossy"?'

- Basic systemic questions, e.g. 'what did the other people say and do?' 'How does that person see you?' 'What would they say about this?'

Other approaches to narrative

See Chapter 27 for some complex approaches to narrative involving writing by the client.

18

Exploring metaphors and blended reactions

Given that metaphors and blends seem deeply involved in our experience of emotion and suffering (Rhodes and Jakes, 2004; Rhodes and Smith, 2010), then it is not surprising to note how the role of metaphors has been important for many therapists from diverse traditions: for example, Cox and Theilgaard (1987), who write from a psychodynamic position, or Sims and Whynot (1997), who described how metaphors are used in systemic therapy. Butler et al. (2008) and also Blenkiron (2010) have explored metaphors in CBT. Metaphor has always been used extensively in narrative therapy (White and Epston, 1990; White, 2007).

A central use of metaphor in therapy is to explore and discover aspects of a person's experience: to illuminate vividly what something feels like, is thought to be, but also what it might imply. Metaphors are rich in meaning, and often say or suggest more than a person realizes at the moment of utterance.

Some clients use metaphors quite spontaneously: these automatic metaphors seem used almost without reflection, and can easily pass without being noticed unless a therapist is very attentive to what is said. A client might, for example, use a phrase such as 'I feel like I am being punished'. It might be suitable at some point, though not necessarily when just said, to refer back to this statement and ask questions such as: 'You said you felt you were being punished; how does that feel?'; 'What or who might be doing that to you?'

It is doubtful that general 'rules' can be given for asking for elaborations of metaphors; however, it can be suggested that asking such questions must fit the emotional and social 'tone' of these moments, must be part of the purpose of work at that time, and, still harder to specify, must cohere or be consistent with the emerging personality of the client.

85

There can be occasions when therapists themselves think up and use explicit metaphors. On the whole, however, NCBT tends to agree with Sims and Whynot (1997) that client-generated metaphors are the ones most likely to resonate with the client, and are the ones that lead to the most useful therapeutic ideas.

Another way of finding metaphors is either explicitly to ask the client during the session or to ask the client to write metaphors between sessions. A simple one-page sheet can be used with the following statements.

- Today, I feel things are like (a)…
- Today, I feel like (a)…
- When I was in a difficult situation today the other person (or people) seemed like (a)…

The sheet is explained: if the client is not sure what a metaphor is, examples can be given from well-known lyrics or poems. For example, 'you are the sunshine of my life' could be suggested and the client asked what this might mean: why was 'sunshine' chosen to stand for life, good feelings, happiness? It can then be useful to ask for an example of a metaphor there and then in the room. These sheets, and variations on them, may be given to a client during the first assessment stage, or can be used at other stages as appropriate.

Some clients particularly like using these sheets and seem to express their feelings better in this manner. One client returned with the following written statements:

- The difficult situation was like they were going to stone me.
- I felt like I was Mary Magdalene.

She said she was not sure what these meant; they had just occurred to her. However, she had said several times that she thought others were talking about her in public and the police might be watching. I wondered with her if being talked about felt like being 'stoned' or being attacked by a group or mob?

I found the image of being 'stoned' quite terrible and felt I could then understand a little better the fear and dread she must feel in going about her daily life. She was not expressing this clearly in literal language, and had a tendency to change topics or resort to humour. With this client the discussion of the metaphor then led to a very emotional discussion of what her life was feeling like and of what she suffered on a daily basis. She became very tearful in expressing these ideas.

The use of metaphor, described above, is mainly for the exploration of possible meanings. The metaphors seem to tell us more than basic talk, to hint at other meanings, yet it is important in NCBT to stay with meanings the client provides and understands. The work must stay within the experiential world of the client and not move into unsupported interpretations.

If the focus of work with the above client became one of encouraging her to do activities in public places (and the metaphor was not a one-off disowned by her later) then it might form a part of a piece of extended therapeutic work. The client could be asked if further public visits feel like 'being stoned'; what helps to make her feel safe, to keep away the stones, or protect herself from such experiences?

Another area of exploration might have been the other possible meanings of this metaphor: for example, is this metaphoric image taken from the Bible? Does it indicate the client's belief that others are being moralistic about her, are judging her about something, perhaps from the past? Such a link was possible since on several occasions she had indicated that she thought others knew about her intimate life but also that she was not working and that they believed she ought to be. The meaning of this metaphor might lead to a narrative exploration of how this started; what were her early experiences of feeling that she was the target of attack?

Metaphoric reactions

As argued, certain extreme reactions of clients can be thought of as being metaphoric or blended reactions. As a homework task one client was trying to go to a gym. His main fear was being looked at. Just before entering the building he had the thought, 'they're going to kill me', though he did not believe this literally and in fact was not prone to paranoid thinking. We explored how it was 'as if' he was about to be attacked and humiliated, and this in turn led to a discussion of similar feelings in the past whilst at school. The work here therefore managed to separate out the two blended elements of fear of going to the gym, and fear of a gang attack.

Positive metaphors

Exploring metaphors can also be useful for goals, desired positive changes and thinking of a preferred future. If a client has shown interest in using metaphors, then a question can be asked, such as: if that occurred, what metaphors could you give for how you would feel? One client had made many good changes: I asked how this felt and he replied that it was like 'healing' and that he felt as if his 'laces were being tied', that is, as if his shoes were now secure and he could move forward in life.

In sum, metaphors arise quite naturally as clients talk, but one can also explicitly ask for examples. They seem to give access to meaning that might not be easily available in everyday literal talk. They are very expressive and can lead to imaginative exploration of ideas. They can tell us a great deal about the actual lived experience of difficulties.

19

Case conceptualization

It is sometimes said that a formulation is absolutely essential: yet it appears that perfectly good therapy proceeds with completely different systems of 'formulation', and some with apparently none at all, as in solution-focused therapy. When CBT experts were asked to give formulations for specific cases, the results were not consistent. Clients are also sometimes distressed by formulations (see Kuyken et al. 2009, for a review).

The position I would like to advocate here is that it is in fact useful in working with most clients to attempt the conceptualization of problems, though there may be situations where it may not be useful (some types of emergency) and, whatever ideas we generate, we need to be modest about their validity. Furthermore, we need first to construct a descriptive conceptualization whose aim is essentially to summarize in one account the main problematic features and relevant psychological aspects which may contribute in different ways to the creation and maintenance of the difficulty. Only later, and if needed, should there be an attempt at giving any type of explanation. For some clients, however, it is useful to map out events over adult years that may have made a contribution, and sometimes, where really needed, to trace difficulties to childhood.

Case conceptualizations can be of 'the problem', but can also address a person's resources and exceptions to the problem (Rhodes and Jakes, 2009). One can ask: what led to this person's ability to cope in such difficult circumstances?

The framework

There are different types and many potential elements in an NCBT conceptualization. Here I wish to suggest the usefulness of thinking in terms of the following possible areas:

- Manifest thoughts, beliefs, narratives, feelings, behaviours (deliberate and habitual), motivations and goals occurring in problematic and usually repeating sequences in specific contexts;
- Networks of specific meanings, metaphors and narratives;
- A repertoire of habitual or reactive dispositions. At any point in time, most are dormant and only some are activated. We can hypothesize certain dispositions exist only by their manifestation in the past;
- For some extreme difficulties, as in psychosis, there may also be the need to understand the person's states of consciousness such as the ability to concentrate, to conduct a coherent conversation and even to have a sense of self over time;
- The above are assumed to have evolved in complex interpersonal and social situations over long periods of time. In some types of NCBT, the history of these would be explored.

Writing a narrative conceptualization

Conceptualizations can be written out in several ways. One way is to write a condensed summary in the form of a simple narrative. The alternative style is to use some sort of diagrammatic representation or picture.

These accounts need to be co-constructed, put together over time by therapist and client in dialogue. The language used should reflect phrases used by the client. The client can be asked to think about such accounts and to write one out at home. In the end the ideas the client constructs will have most long-term effect.

Case illustration: Sally

Work with Sally will be described over several chapters (each case illustration in the book is a fictional reconstruction from several cases, with details altered for anonymity). Sally presented with long-term depression, sometimes outbursts of fear, difficulties getting on with others in public, an attitude of self-hate or disgust and a sort of pessimism about life. She reported having a stable childhood with good family relationships. She had, however, been the victim of years of domestic violence in her 20s. Fortunately, she left this man and had a son with another man, who left soon after. She came to therapy just after the death of an uncle, but was preoccupied with memories of the death of her older sister when Sally was nine years old.

A very simple and early descriptive formulation to share was as follows:

> You are feeling depressed. If something goes well, you tend to tell yourself, 'you will pay for it'. You often feel hate and even disgust about yourself. This stops you getting to know other people and keeps you from doing what you would like to do with your son such as go swimming and shopping.
>
> We wondered if this attitude of hate started in the years of domestic abuse you suffered.
>
> In spite of all this you love and look after your son and keep the house in perfect condition. You also have one trusted friend.

Greater depth and narrative detail were added to the above over different phases of therapy, particularly after work on the two major traumas (see Chapter 22).

A diagrammatic overview for Sally is given in Figure 19.1. It shows three repetitive problem sequences and a selection of potential dispositions and narrations. While this conceptualization focuses on specific sequences, alternative versions could have described life-long developments.

Diagrams

I personally really enjoy thinking with a flow chart, but many clients do not. I think we need to be sensitive and not to assume giving visual display is useful. For some it is very informative; for others, not at all. If visual aids are used then perhaps it is best if they are kept

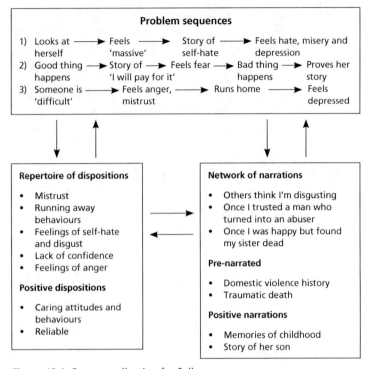

Figure 19.1 Conceptualization for Sally.

very simple. Figure 19.1 would have been intimidating for Sally: for her I hand-drew very specific pictures to emphasize in later work a contrast between the negative way of living and a preferred way.

Sharing the conceptualization

In general it is helpful to share a conceptualization with the client. However, there certainly are several situations where that is not a good idea (see Kuyken et al., 2009, for a review). For some clients tracing problems back to childhood is upsetting and in short-term work is often not needed. With psychosis the very form of a conceptualization suggests a psychological problem whereas quite often that is not how clients at first see their difficulties; for example, from the client's point of view the fear that demons are coming is not a problem of misinterpretation, but something real and external. For some psychotic clients it can be better to start with a modest and focused description; for example, that the stress the person has suffered has led to an increase in the symptoms. Over time, other more complex versions can be offered and discussed if needed.

20

Solution-focused exploration

When to use an SF approach?

Solution-focused work is particularly useful as a first therapeutic approach in situations and problem presentations that are 'messy' or 'unstable', or where something needs to be done quickly due to safety concerns. It is, however, an approach that could be used at any point: typically I would tend to use it early in work, but might return to it several times as new issues arise, or simply as a reminder of what has helped.

The fundamental stance

As discussed earlier, I think the key feature, as Bliss and Bray (2009) argue, is the stance of building solutions from those 'materials' the client brings. Sometimes the client might actually have a good 'solution' but needs encouragement and confidence. Most typically, however, a solution is generated in a complex dialogue, where 'clues' are thought about, exceptions to the problem discussed and a picture of the future is imagined.

Questions and tasks

The various writers in the SF tradition have provided a sort of basic 'tool kit' of possible questions and tasks, and these questions and tasks are used to explore the following key topics.

1. What is the problem pattern? How is it described?
2. Are there exceptions to the problem, and if so, can they be utilized by the client?

3. What are the client's goals? In particular, what is the 'phenomenology' of these goals? How will the realization of those goals be experienced by the client, and how does the client express these in words?
4. If there are no utilizable exceptions, can a 'solution' be imagined? By 'solution' here is meant some idea or behaviour that might help the person in his or her attempt to move toward goals.
5. How do any of the above 'fit' the person's 'lived world', his or her relationships or interpersonal 'systems'? What will others see and do? How does this help or not help?

Exploring the above further one can ask:

- For exceptions: If there are times the problem does not occur, what is different about those times? How did you manage not to do *x*?
- Goals: What would be a first sign of success? What would that look like?
- What changes do you want in your life?
- Hypothetical futures: If the problem was solved, how would you know? How would your life be different? Who would notice first?
- Scaling questions: Where ten equals that good life you described and one the worst things ever were, where are you now?

There is no set order for these questions: the specific link from topic to topic is improvised according to the flow of dialogue. Whatever the pathway, clarification is needed for all these areas.

Towards the end of a session a session break can be very useful: the therapist explains beforehand that he or she will leave the room to read through the notes taken, and think how to proceed. On return, compliments are often given to the client. The session may end with questions to consider and sometimes tasks are negotiated.

Tasks for the client

At the end of a session, the following can be suggested:

- Noticing tasks: Notice what you do when you overcome the urge to x (have an argument).
- Appreciation tasks: Write down what you appreciate or value about your present life, self, relationships, etc.
- Do more of what works: You mentioned x might help. Could you do more of that?
- Do something different: Next time the fixed pattern we discussed happens, why not try something different, however small?

Solution-focused conceptualizing

De Shazer and colleagues do not produce formulations of the problem, but de Shazer has illustrated the planning and thinking that sometimes go on outside the session. Combining the latter with ideas in this book, then some possible questions for therapists to consider are:

- Has a full picture emerged? Can it be considered a rich description?
- If 'exceptions' are described, why has the client not already done more of these? What may be blocking this? Is it useful to suggest doing more, or should one be more tentative?
- It is useful to think of 'exceptions' as occurring at different 'levels' of the problem, from the very concrete and behavioural to levels concerning attitudes to change and the experience of confidence and trust. Which type has been described?
- If getting stuck, have you the 'the right problem', or a really useful description of the problem?
- If really stuck, is it time for you to do something different?
- Does the client use a 'global frame', that is, a fixed way of reinterpreting everything that happens such that it always fits the frame. Accepting the frame as true, what would the implications be? Do the assumptions of the client in fact lead to implications the clients themselves would find puzzling or unacceptable? For example, de Shazer (1988) wondered with one client: given you said the FBI were ruthless and efficient assassins, I wonder why they have not succeeded over many years?

The narrative solution-focused therapists Eron and Lund (1996), however, did use conceptualizations that summarized negative cycles of doing and viewing in contrast to potential positive doing and viewing cycles.

Constructive sequences of work

The questions concerning goals or exceptions are not meant to be asked in isolation, one at a time. A 'question' can take up a whole session and will involve a complex sequence of questions and responses (Lipchik, 2002).

While some SF therapy involves few sessions, with more diffi-cult clients the work can extend over many sessions, and can some-times be 'intermitted', that is, extended with many breaks over years (Lipchik, 2002). The client may struggle with an extreme problem such as fear of others, and the solutions may have to be discussed many times for these to be absorbed into the person's way of living.

SFT and hope

The areas explored in SFT can be realized in many ways, and one version of SFT (Ratner et al., 2012) has the following emphasis and general sequence: first clients are asked 'what are your best hopes from therapy?' The therapist then moves on to asking what differ-ences it would make to the person if these hopes were realized? Next the therapist explores if any 'instances' of the hoped-for life have occurred, now or in the past.

Combining SF work with a behavioural focus

I have found that for some clients it is useful to fuse SF work with ideas taken from behavioural activation, activity scheduling and exposure work. This combination is very useful if ideas have not been generated from what the client has given. For example, if an agreed aim is to confront fear and walk to the local shop, then one can explain how many clients have found that taking small steps and exposing oneself to the fear involved, but under control, has helped. If this makes sense, the client is invited to try. As the client starts to practise such steps, one can add to this by asking further SF questions, such as: Yesterday, you managed to do this task; how in fact did you prepare yourself for that step? What helped you to cope with the fear? What worked?

Case illustration: Sally

Asking Sally the hypothetical future question was difficult: 'I can't imagine it' was her first response, followed by long silence. Slowly, however, after further discussion she was able to make very tentative suggestions:

- 'Going out ... not feeling scared';
- 'Just enjoying the moment'.

    Next week she came back with:

- 'Live in a house, with a white wooden fence and a garden'.

Who would notice any changes? Her son, who would see her going swimming, cooking, shopping, and even going to the cinema.

When I went on to discuss her goals she listed the activities above, and to do more with her son, not to feel depressed, and to have more self-confidence.

I explored potential exceptions, that is, when did she ever feel better and not hate herself? A major recent exception was 'having a joke with her son'.

Sally was asked to do the 'what do you value in your life ... etc.' task. She managed to list several things:

- Her son;
- She had one good friend;
- Lots of good memories from childhood. She recounted episodes of cooking with her mother and the kindness of her father.

These areas and what they said about her values in life were returned to many times.

As work proceeded initiatives were reported: she had overcome her fear and taken her son to visit a new school. After forgetting her wristwatch she managed to keep thinking 'I've just forgotten it' and not engage in an explosion of self-hate. Another time she took her son to the cinema. The session ended with me giving her compliments on how the dedication to her son was strong and how she struggled to do things for him in spite of her suffering.

The upshot of this phase was the articulation of a valued exception and renewed commitment to engaging in difficult activities such as going to public places.

21

Constructional and structured approaches to self-beliefs

There have been several approaches developed within CBT which have explicitly worked with negative ideas or beliefs about the self but have also made the building of new positive beliefs a key focus. In this chapter I shall illustrate the work of Padesky, Korrelbloom and Tarrier.

The preferred self

Padesky (1994) presents a method for working with core beliefs of the self which relies on working with strengths and the consideration of new possibilities.

Assessment

The client is presented with a range of incomplete statements and asked to give suggestions. The first set of sentences is:

*   I am …
*   People are …
*   The world is …

    A fourth possible statement I add sometimes is:

*   Other people think I am …

These sentences are not just presented, but negotiated with the client. Most clients give negative statements spontaneously, but if not, then it can be appropriate to ask if the client holds any negative ideas or doubts in specific difficult situations. For example:

- When things do not go well, what do you think of yourself?
- If there are certain moments you don't like yourself, then how would you complete that sentence at that time?

Similar prompting can be carried out for sentences concerning others.

During this phase it is useful to write the replies down and ask: how much do you believe this out of 100%? A record can be kept over several weeks.

The next phase is to begin to ask the person to complete the sentences:

- I prefer to be …
- I prefer people to be …
- I prefer the world to be …
- I prefer that others think about me that I am …

Some answer with little hesitation, but with some clients, the process is much more difficult. Again, it is useful to obtain several answers, discuss which are most important and ask for how much the preferred belief is believed to be true out of 100%.

Positive data log

In the first session of doing this work, I usually suggest completing a positive data log as follows: a completed sentence, in particular, 'I prefer to be …' is written at the top of a piece of paper, and then the client is asked if they can think of any examples. If none are suggested, then I normally suggest one, and hopefully, one that is convincing to the client, such as, 'You are a very reliable person; you always turn up on time'. The client is asked to take the sheet home and look out for more examples, and to bring it next week for discussion. This can be built on over several weeks.

Historic record

Another useful method is to write the statement about self on a piece of paper at the top, and along the side write out age bands, such as 0 to 2, 2 to 5, 5 to 11, etc. One can then look for examples at different times in a person's life.

Sometimes I write both the negative and positive statements at the top: this can be very useful in that there is often nothing in the person's early life that the client believes is very negative. It is a great pleasure to watch clients realize that there was nothing terrible about their younger selves, that they were not a 'monster' at age two.

The competitive memory training (COMET) approach

Korrelboom and associates (2010) have taken the model of change suggested by Brewin (see Chapter 11) and developed a programme which can be used in conjunction with CBT or other therapies. COMET can be presented in groups or one to one. Their approach is very much focused on being constructional and also involves writing narratives.

COMET involves several steps: first identifying a negative self-image, then developing at least a credible positive self-image in contrast; a next step is to strengthen the positive images, to make these more vivid and memorable (see below); finally the client practises the new image to obtain a feeling of confidence, then imagines a difficult situation while trying to carry into this picture the prior confident feeling.

Four main methods are used to strengthen the positive image:

1. Clients are asked to write small stories about themselves that show how the positive qualities have been or could be shown in everyday situations; for example, if clients had said they were kind, to write about an episode showing this quality.
2. Clients are asked to visualize themselves in scenarios where they are showing the relevant positive qualities.

3.   The therapist suggests putting or holding the body and face in ways consistent with the desired qualities, for example, having a confident upright posture, looking around at others.
4.   Clients are encouraged to find encouraging music, consistent with their positive image, and to play this before trying a targeted difficult situation.

Several evaluations by Korrelboom and associates (2010) suggest that there are positive changes in aspects of self-esteem and in levels of depression for clients with personality disorders, clinical depression and other types of difficulties, including hearing voices and eating disorders.

Korrelboom et al. discuss the issue of whether their approach actually improves 'self-esteem' or something else, such as 'self-acceptance': there may of course be other possibilities. It seems to be possible that in fact the main change is one of confidence itself (as described in Chapter 9).

Monitoring positive behaviour

Hall and Tarrier (2003) describe a method whereby psychotic patients were asked to generate positive qualities about themselves and to strengthen these descriptions by making autobiographic memories as specific as possible. A homework task was to monitor their behaviour over the week and to record specific evidence to support the positive self-statements. Results suggested several improvements in self-esteem, psychotic symptoms and social functioning at three-month follow-up.

Overview

Within CBT itself various approaches, as described here, have been developed that focus on building a new and positive picture of the self and are highly compatible with work done in an NCBT framework.

22

Trauma

Working with traumas

Many clients report various types of traumas in their lives, and for many of these it is fairly obvious that the traumas are not 'past' and forgotten, but influence in various ways their present everyday lives. These effects range from classic symptoms of posttraumatic stress disorder, such as reliving, to more complex effects, for example, a client who had been abused heard a 'voice' telling others about her past.

In working with trauma it is essential to differentiate single-episode trauma from prolonged and complex trauma (Herman, 1992). For single-episode traumas, such as a car accident, it might be best to use standard CBT methods such as exposure and the challenging of 'hot spots' (Ehlers and Clark, 2000). Alternatively, one can take ideas from Meichenbaum (1994), who developed constructive NCBT for both single and complex traumas. He advocated listening to the trauma in depth, then finding ways of normalizing the person's reactions, of validating their experiences, and highlighting areas of strength.

The work in this chapter will look at a method for complex traumas.

Suitable clients

On the whole I think trauma-focused work should only be attempted where there are clear and obvious effects of the trauma; where the client has spontaneously mentioned their traumatic experience and keeps returning to this topic; and where the client very clearly wishes to do this work. The therapist must also consider the well-being and safety of the client, that is, to consider if it is a good moment for such work, whether the client might benefit or not, and if it should be done at all.

Method of therapy

One of the first major therapies for the victims of torture was developed by Chilean psychologists after the military coup in the 1970s (Cienfuegos and Monelli, 1983). This work had its origin in the writing of fully detailed histories or testimonies by survivors, with the aim of sending those to the United Nations. The psychologists found, however, that the act of retelling and recording a written account had beneficial psychological effects. Telling the story of trauma might be traced further back to several other early innovators (see Herman, 1992, for a review). The method of testimony was taken by Neuner and colleagues (2002) for work with refugees and developed in various ways.

A great number of psychotic patients report trauma and abuse (Read et al., 2004). A colleague and I therefore adapted the above, adding ideas from narrative solution-focused therapy (NSFT). This is the approach I shall outline here. I have used it with psychotic patients and those with chronic mood disorders (see Chapter 29).

When to focus on trauma

This work is not suitable in the early stages of therapy, and should not be attempted until at least assessment and solution-focused or behavioural work on coping have been completed, and a strong therapeutic alliance has been established.

Narrative therapy for trauma

Like other trauma work, it is essential that it is well discussed beforehand, and that the rationale is fully understood. The client must be in control and have choice (Herman, 1992).

There are many 'routes' or paths one could take, and these must be designed according to the needs of the unique client. One general sequence for complex trauma is to cover the following areas:

- Ask the client to relate their account of the difficulties, beginning if possible before the trauma began. This is described to the client as giving a general overview of what happened, and if required, that it may be useful to focus on specific outstanding moments at a subsequent stage.
- The attitude of the therapist needs to be attentive, to be a witness, to record and write down details and to express compassion as felt and as appropriate.
- Having covered the major negative events the client wishes to discuss, at that point it can be useful to step back and, if appropriate, simply to acknowledge the extremity of what has occurred. Sometimes it can be useful to think about possible connections over time (what was heard at the time and is now heard in nightmares).
- A next stage is to explain that it might be useful to consider any good areas of a person's life and times when things have gone well. Here there may be a need to prompt; for example, if it is known that the person has worked, or had friends, to ask if these were good things in the person's life. This should not be a 'forced' activity.
- Towards the end of these stages, it is useful to write a letter. This will summarize the main difficulties and possible effects, but also list and comment on exceptions and strengths.

Building the alternative story

Besides direct asking and remembering of good or better times, as above, other methods of building an alternative narrative include:

- Exploration of ideas found in a prior solution-focused phase;
- The expression of a compassionate alternative to negative ideas about self (see Chapter 23);
- The use of 'unique outcome' questions for identity (see Chapter 24).

Sally and trauma work

For Sally there were two major areas of trauma: one, the death of her sister and the other, many years of domestic violence.

Her sister had died in a bicycle accident. Sally had been told to get in the car so they could visit her in hospital. In the car she laughed and joked with her brother. When they got there, her sister was already dead. Sally attacked herself for laughing on the way.

As we went through the details of the funeral, she remembered how she thought that her dead sister could not 'breathe', that she was 'alone' and 'trapped'.

After recounting this we were able to have a discussion about the nature of a dead body, how according to her religion the 'spirit' would have left.

Following White, I then did work on what her sister would think of her continuing to attack herself, and what contribution they had made to each other's lives.

The work on domestic violence followed the narrative exposure therapy model: we constructed an account of how this had begun and how her partner had manipulated her. We looked at selected episodes of violence and how she had eventually escaped. This produced a range of emotions, including anger at her 'own stupidity'.

After the abuse narratives, the main aim was to construct a sort of 'counter' story, that is, a non-blaming account of how she had been captured by her partner, one that emphasized her innocence and trust, as opposed to 'stupidity', as she had suggested. I was able to put her life history in the wider sociological context of violent men who combine 'charm' with tyranny and how many women are exploited like her.

If a positive life history has not been done, then it should be considered after recounting trauma. For Sally we had already done this in the SF phase and therefore were able to draw on it as an inspiration for values, in particular the core purpose of looking after her son.

Of course this chapter is not sufficient for working with trauma and only the briefest outline has been given of how this therapy is carried out. Those wishing to learn, I believe, will need to attend relevant workshops and have expert supervision.

23

Building alternative meanings

NCBT does not use as its main method direct cognitive challenging, yet there are specific topics where questioning a negative idea or exploring alternative ideas may play a useful role. This chapter looks at three of these methods.

Exploring alternative perspectives

This approach can be useful for a limited period with some clients, particularly if it is not clear what the relevant themes are that occur in difficult situations. I explain that there are many ways of looking at a situation and some may be more helpful than others. There is no attempt to dispute the client's original negative thoughts. The following is presented as a sheet that the client is asked to fill in at home:

* Describe what happened when distressed (other areas can be specified).
* What did you think and feel and do?

    The following can be added after a couple of weeks:

* Is there an alternative way of looking at this situation?

    The answers should be discussed without any insistence on a particular way of viewing the situation. If no alternatives are given, the topic could be returned to after further work on new narratives.

Presenting a compassionate alternative view

A client had witnessed as a child secret traumatic family events which he had not been able to stop. From our discussion it was obvious that the weight of this was somehow crushing for him. A useful question at the point was:

• What did you conclude from these events?'

Lee (2005) suggests this question when collecting information from clients concerning how they have been treated by their parents when young. My client made several comments, but most striking was that he was 'a coward', and that it meant he was an utterly 'bad person'. At such a point there is a choice for therapists; that is, just to witness what has been said, or make some kind of commentary or response. However, if some commentary is made, it does not have to be a direct challenge or Socratic questioning. The therapist can state a personal and compassionate view, or just 'think out loud' to open possible questions that can be returned to at a later time. This is, in fact, to enter into a dialogue.

For this client I thought it useful if I did state a position and at least to open up some questions. I said I did not judge him in such a way and reminded him that at the time he was only about nine years old. He cried, and later told me he had not done that for years.

Whereas challenging or questioning a belief intellectually rarely seems sufficient, it does seem more powerful if done at a moment of intense emotion, during a dramatic telling of a person's deepest secrets and fears.

Deconstructing the taken-for-granted

A strength of narrative therapy in particular is that it has always paid attention to the role of culture and society in the thinking about problems. White and Epston (1990) drew upon the ideas of Foucault, arguing that in the discourses of society some things are represented as 'normal' and people attempt to fit in with these norms or prescriptions for ways of living; however, a person may not fit the norm, for example, of success or gender role behaviour.

Whether Foucault's theories are correct or not, there are many reported clinical examples of how people suffer with regard to society's norms and stereotypes. Sometimes this is explicit, but often the effect is indirect. The person engages in a certain way of behaving, for example, a version of masculine behaviour, or states a 'truth', such as 'men should fight to succeed', and these are 'taken for granted', are thought of as 'natural', the way things just are and must be.

Three very common constrictive norms revolve around the topics of:

1. Being a 'man' or 'woman';
2. Being a 'perfect mother';
3. Being a 'success'.

Some possible questions with which to explore these areas are:

- How did you develop the idea of 'success'? Where do you think this might have come from in your childhood or adult years? Did you choose this idea or was it absorbed without you realizing?
- How do you judge people who are successful in contrast to those who are not?
- Why is it important? If you had this, how would you be different?
- Is this ideal helping you in your life or is it a constriction?
- What would be an alternative ideal? How would you live if you followed that new ideal?

The aim of deconstructing such rigid stereotypes and practice is not to tell the client what is right or wrong, but rather to invite the client to become aware of these patterns, to wonder about their origins and to decide whether they are actually wanted or unwanted now in their life.

24

Identity, values and purpose

In this chapter the focus shifts in working with narratives of 'identity', of what the person hopes for, prefers to be and become, and what values are given importance. Of course, the topics of actions and identity interconnect and overlap, but in therapy, for clarity, it can help to focus more on one than the other at different stages. White (2007) has been very creative in this area and designed many approaches. Here I present only a few ideas taken from White and somewhat modified to fit the NCBT frame.

Noticing unique outcomes

In earlier stages of therapy, when the client is describing difficulties, it is very useful at least to note for later use any mention of times the problems did not occur, or simply times and events in the person's life when things may have gone well. Of particular interest are times when the person appears to have deliberately engaged in actions which seem constructive and which may have been efforts to make personal changes.

One might therefore notice exceptions and initiatives during the problem narration in the early phases of therapy, or one can make a deliberate decision to look for exceptions at a later stage. For example, after a person has described traumatic events it can be a very useful moment to wonder about times when things have been better.

Whilst it can be very difficult with some clients to locate exceptions, it is surprising how often many clients do mention them, or begin to, as therapy progresses. One client recently quite spontaneously told me how that week she had refused something she normally would have just put up with. It was a surprising new behaviour for her. This provided a great opportunity for exploration.

One approach for discovering the values of a person and connecting these to constructive narratives is exploring the following.

Giving the unique outcome a name

If an exception is mentioned, it can be explored:

* Tell me more about that.
* Can you describe how you did this? How did you prepare for this step?
* Was it surprising to you?
* Can you give this action a name? What phrase or metaphor captures what happened?

Mapping the effects of the exception

* What effect did this have upon you?
* How did you feel at the time and afterwards?
* What happened next?
* How did others react? What did others notice?

Evaluating the exception and effects

* Do you welcome the fact you carried out this action?
* Is this something you would like to do more of or have in your life?

Explaining the evaluation

* Why do you welcome this exception, this change?
* Why is 'standing up for yourself' a good thing? What is it about it that you like?

- If you chose to do more of this sort of behaviour, is it something that fits with what you want in life? Does it fit the values you have about life? Do you know where these values come from? Who might help you develop these values?
- Given that you do want more 'independence' in your life and no longer want to be a person who accepts unpleasant demands, what new actions might you think of doing to move in that direction ?

The above examples must be altered to fit the concepts and language of the person.

Elaborating and deepening the new narrative of self

Over time the client is encouraged to articulate a new narrative of the future and a characterization of self: this work goes straight to the heart of a person's 'projects', their intentions and plans for the future. It is therefore deeply motivational: it aims to rekindle lost motivations or to create new ones.

Having elaborated a new narrative of self, from that point on the work can focus on thinking of new ways of bringing into existence the preferred picture. There can be an extended focus on new ways of being in context. The new narrative can also be better established, and can be given more weight and depth, by employing methods such as asking the client to find people who might support the preferred story and give feedback on new developments.

In the following illustration how the problem was externalized will be explained first (as outlined in Chapter 17), followed by how this led on to unique outcome work.

Externalization of the problem: Sally

Externalizing the problem of 'self-hate' for Sally produced the following sequence. First, she confirmed that 'self-hate' and disgust were good descriptions (she had said them already). She added 'something you would want to walk by and not notice'.

The effect of self-hate was shame; she did not want to be seen. It stopped her doing activities with her son, for example, going to a café for a treat.

She thought these effects were 'bad'. On being asked why,she gave many reasons: 'stop bettering myself', 'letting her down'. She wanted the best for her son, for him to be independent.

Unique outcome and evaluations: Sally

Sally's relation to her son had emerged as a major exception or unique outcome (White, 2007). I asked if there had been anything as good in her life: the answer was no, this was the best thing, a 'blessing'. Next I explored a little how she had prepared for having a child. This revealed an account of resisting her partner's negative attitude, and her wish to have a family.

The effects were many: someone to look after, to care about and to love. Her son made her happy, 'kept me going', and stopped her from 'falling over the edge'.

Why were these good things? She was helping him to be independent, to live. This led to her telling me about the sacrifices her father had made in coming to England, how he would 'go to prison' for his family. She told me he had a good heart. We wondered if her sort of commitment was a continuation of her father's aims in life, what he too had lived for. She was clearly moved.

I next drew out a sheet with two titles: 'What does self-hate make you do?', 'What is the lifestyle of self-hate?' And on another sheet, 'How would you live if following values of care, having a good heart and being true?' 'What is this way of living?'

Overview

I personally do not like the phrase of 're-authoring' the 'self' since a possible misunderstanding is that one could reinvent the past, or make a 'fiction' of oneself and just become it. The version I present here is meant to proceed from real events and real aspirations. It asks the client to notice and elaborate on details that are being ignored or just not seen. These exceptions are there but in a 'pre-narrative' form. For me, the new narrative is a potential truth about a person's life and expresses real hope for the future.

25

Constructional approaches to interaction patterns

For some problems it is useful to maintain a sustained focus, preferably every session for many weeks. Any problem that occurs with high frequency, for example, attacks of fear, can be suitable. This chapter, however, will look in particular at how to work with social difficulties that a client reports occur most weeks, if not every day. There are many sorts of social problems: one very common cluster of problems revolves around fear of others, of withdrawal and of not saying what is on one's mind. Some clients who 'give in' and who do not express themselves later attack themselves for being 'weak' and can spiral down into terrible feelings. The very opposite problem can be one of being too outspoken, aggressive or negative, followed by feeling regret or rejection. Some problems fit no obvious pattern and are complex and idiosyncratic. Social problems, as argued earlier, involve not only beliefs or narrative, but are also utterly entwined with feelings, motivations, confidence, trust, and in the context of the dispositional self.

With some clients after the initial exploration and other work, a focus on one or two specific problems spontaneously emerges. With other clients, however, a direction does not emerge automatically, and in those cases it is sometimes appropriate to negotiate a sustained focus on a specific social problem. The problem suggested, however, must be of obvious relevance to the client, and something they themselves have mentioned as important to change.

Exploring the social problem

If already well discussed, exploration here might be the simple task of checking if there still is a mutual understanding. The problem can

119

be characterized and 'named'. Often, however, it is useful to explore in greater depth both recent examples of the difficulty and the history of this difficulty. To various degrees, this exploration might go back to childhood (see Chapter 26).

One can ask or explore the following:

- Describe a time when this problem occurred.
- Can you describe it in a sequence, that is, before, during and after?
- What did you feel? What did you think? What did you want in the situation?
- Is there a history of these interactions with that person or with others?
- Can you give a metaphor or image of what it felt like?
- Was there a 'blended reaction' at the time (see Chapter 18)?
- Can you show me how the statements were said and in what tone of voice?

The aim here is to understand, to describe in detail.

Exploring alternatives

Next, the client's attitude to the specific problematic interaction needs to be explored and alternatives considered:

- Is this how you wish to be?
- Why do you not wish to be like this? Why is it negative for you?
- How would you have preferred to interact?
- Why would this be something you prefer?
- Would this new way of behaving fit your preferred identity, as we discussed earlier?
- Can you give a metaphor, image or motto for this preferred way of interacting?
- Have you ever acted like this in the past or with others?

If there are exceptions – for example, the person is not confident with a boss, but is with friends – how this comes about can be explored.

Weekly structured analysis

The next phase is to return to this problem area repeatedly, and to think how the person can initiate changes and put these into practice. The practice in real situations is essential. The weekly focus can have the following structure:

1. What went well or not well this week? If there are spontaneous changes, 'initiatives', these are particularly worth exploring.
2. As part of the work, the client can be asked to keep a written record of what has occurred. It can be very useful to give to the client a simple structured sheet for this purpose, including the following areas:
    *   Describe the problem event in sequence.
    *   How did you feel?
3. It is very important to move on to a discussion of the preferred way of interacting:
    *   How would you have preferred to react?
    *   What could make that more likely if a similar situation happens this week?
    *   As therapy progresses, these questions can also be given as a task to try each day.
4. On some occasions it can be useful to plan actual changes, particularly where the problematic situation is easily predicated.
    *   If x occurs, what can you do?

The new behaviour needs to be envisaged and practised: it first needs to be put into words, and for some clients it can also be very useful to practise with visual imagery or role playing (see Chapter 27).

The sustained focus over several weeks is important: negative patterns carried out over years do not just disappear, and the new behaviour needs repeated indepth discussion and practice.

Sally

When Sally experienced any social difficulties she tended to leave the situation, go home, feel upset and attack herself.

We worked to change this pattern in the light of how she would interact if fully committed to her narrative of being kind but strong. During this phase she managed after conflict for the first time not to go home, sit in the café, read a paper and then return to the class.

Over time we were able to work on her going into many situations and not withdrawing, or engaging in self-attacking thoughts.

Overview

The approach in this chapter is a fusion of ideas taken from NSF therapies, but using the more structured framework more typically found in CBT. It shares with McCullough's (2000) approach a sustained concentrated focus on social difficulties. The essence is the continued movement between 'problems' and generating solutions.

26

Working with the unknown self

Exploring the unknown self

Guidano (1991) considered his approach to cognitive therapy as being constructivist. He emphasized that deeply held beliefs are linked to lifelong development and emotion and are not simply changed by a cool logical argument about evidence. He suggested that different types of pathology, such as depression or obsessive-compulsive disorder, could be linked to a person's experience of attachment relationships (Bowlby, 1969). He was a pioneer of linking cognitive therapy to developmental theory. His therapeutic work involved narrating the past: a key technique was to ask a person to remember recent difficult interpersonal situations and, as therapy progressed, to link this to situations with early attachment figures. He asked clients to elaborate the story of what happened in the past from both an 'outside' viewpoint and, in contrast, from the 'inside' viewpoint. There are now, of course, several approaches within the family of CBT therapies that examine the present in terms of a person's early experience. One such system is Young's schema therapy (Young et al., 2003).

In contrast to Young or Guidano, the work in this book tends to be focused on using 'near-experience' descriptions. That is, when building the narrative of a problem and its solution, where possible, there is an attempt to stay with a client's everyday language and use little explanatory theory other than what might emerge quite naturally in everyday talk, and in general to stay in the present or recent times. There are, however, some presentations which do profit from an investigation into the distant past and where there is need to make sense of the connection of meaning or causation over time.

Making connections over time

In many cases, as a story of recent suffering unfolds, possible connections between the onset of a difficulty and the present begin to be seen. A client may state at the beginning: I really cannot see why I became depressed last year or why I have panic attacks now. But as one explores what has just happened in the life of the person, usually in the year before onset, it soon becomes obvious that the events and their meaning are clear and deeply connected. More importantly, the client spontaneously sees and discusses these connections: they might say, 'I've never just sat down and thought about all this.'

In contrast to the above, some symptoms and their meaning are not at all obvious to the client: they are baffling, 'out the blue', and do not seem clearly linked to current events or to any events before onset. Furthermore, the meaning does not become clear after further questioning by the therapist: there seems to be no obvious link between how this problem is triggered and events that are occurring. If the client is very interested and willing to explore such problems then, as in the tradition of Guidano, I find it can be useful to explore at least briefly early events; that is, to see if current problems link to something that occurred in childhood.

Case illustration

One client reported that for many years she was on occasion overwhelmed by a sense of terror and dread: however, it was also striking that she reported it as not linked to ongoing events of any type, and that it was marked by a strong feeling of nausea. After basic work on anxiety and mindfulness meditation training, these attacks still seemed incomprehensible. A thought record suggested anxious thinking, but this did not seem linked to the attacks.

It was decided to explore the attacks by tracing them back to their earliest occurrence. The client was asked to close her eyes and remember the feeling of nausea and fear as it occurred in childhood. Several episodes of intense anxiety were remembered, for example, around house chores. Eventually, however, episodes of being told off were recalled, and she distinctly remembered having to wait for her 'punishment', but that it would occur after the evening meal. She had no appetite and felt sick with fear. The client had never thought about these connections to the past.

I made no effort to persuade the client that there must be a link. The client considered this straightaway.

I did, however, as part of a new conceptualization, discuss with the client how:

- Early events can cause deep, long-standing memories;
- Not all memory is accessible, all the time, to our conscious mind;
- Something may be forgotten, yet it can influence our feelings. It leaves a 'pattern in the brain', and this neurological pattern can be activated without deliberate awareness.

The explanatory framework, is of course, borrowed from theories of emotion and memory as found in LeDoux (1998) and Schacter (1996), and uses the framework outlined earlier, that is, the difference between accessible thoughts in a network of narrations as opposed to habitual and reactive dispositions. Due to the repeated exposure to a disturbing type of situation in her childhood, she was left with a disposition to have explosive feelings of fear associated with sickness, and a disposition that could be easily triggered by events where she was not aware of meaningful connections.

I have recently used a similar explanatory structure with a client who suffers a chronic conviction that he smells. It was possible to make a direct thematic link between the nature of the present smell and highly unpleasant events he was exposed to in childhood.

Overview

Narrative can be combined with a developmental emphasis and one early pioneer was the cognitive therapist Guidano. The latter's work has been developed by Arciero and Bondolfi (2011). Narrative and attachment are also creatively combined in the family therapy of Dallos (2006).

While understanding is rarely sufficient to change a pattern, not to understand is in itself a torment for clients and sometimes leads to self-attacking attempts to explain what these reactions might imply. Constructing a narrative of onset leads to understanding and more creative ways of dealing with the persistent difficulty.

27

Working with images, enactment and writing

The methods in this chapter can not only be used to explore problems, but are also very useful in the construction of new ideas and to 'enrich' (Morgan, 2000) the new narration.

Imagery

The use of imagery in psychotherapy, where one might actually experience in imagination either difficulties, or alternatively, coping and more benign ways of responding, has a long and complex history (Hackmann et al., 2011). The latter book is a rich source of ideas and practices, of which many aim to be constructional.

Solution-orientated therapies also have a long history of using imagery. One of the most well-known techniques in SFT, the 'miracle question', was in fact a development from a technique where the client was asked to visualize a future life without difficulties, but also to imagine how this might be achieved in a series of steps (de Shazer, 1985, p. 81).

The following are techniques that can be used flexibly at diverse stages of therapy.

Visualizing a preferred future

A standard technique in SFT is to initiate a conversation about a preferred future. In the course of doing this, if the client is stuck, it is sometimes useful to ask a client to close their eyes, given they are comfortable about doing this. If the client does not wish to close their eyes the work can be done with eyes open (perhaps looking at a wall) and then the client imagines their future life without the specific problem.

- What would you be doing?
- What is the expression on your face? How do others respond?
- What happens next?

For some clients is it is useful to ask: what would I see on a video if these changes occurred? What will you be doing differently? When the problem is solved, what will I see others doing (Rowan and O'Hanlon, 1999)?

Besides specific situations, as above, one can ask the client to imagine a story of change unfolding over many episodes.

Visualizing the past

In the approach of Guidano (see Chapter 26), there is an emphasis on actually visualizing past events, in particular as a way of changing long-held rigid and dysfunctional explanations of the past. Gonçalves (1994) suggested seeing a difficult event from the 'outside', then again from the 'inside', and then went on to explore metaphors for the event.

Constructing a new image

Hackmann et al. (2011) have described constructional work where clients with upsetting images can be asked actively to transform the image in benign ways. For some clients imagining something quite surreal, even humorous, can be effective.

Image work: Sally

As Sally went out more, she began to feel that the abuser was about, watching her in public places. She often had images of this man coming into her mind. One piece of work was to go through exactly what she could do if he saw her or approached her in reality.

At a follow-up stage she reported an image of a man attacking her and 'chopping' at her head. It 'hung off' and she struggled to speak.

I asked her to imagine me and the police coming to stop him and chasing him off. We also did a separate exercise where she accessed the image of her chopped head and reversed this so she could see how her head was healed and fine.

Enactments

Enactment, role play, skill rehearsal, that is, where a person does not just talk 'about' something, but performs the action in the room, also has a long history (Mahoney, 2003). Some forms of enactment are quite demanding, but many versions can be 'gentle' and carried out for a few moments: for example, one might simply ask a client to just 'say what you will say to your boss'.

Where possible, it can be very useful actually to observe the negative way of reacting and behaving as it occurs in a public place, for example, how someone with fear of others walks in the street. In this situation, one can simply go for a walk with the client or visit a busy place such as the local shops. After the observation, back in the office, one can then develop with the client a conception of a preferred way of behaving. Next, the client can be asked to try at least a small part of that whilst in the room. It may be useful to combine this with visualization before practice.

Writing: letters, writing and documents

The use of writing by clients and various types of documents are very useful ways of encouraging the exploration of difficulties and the building of new narratives and solutions. These methods, however, will not be suitable for those who find literacy challenging, or who for whatever reason have a strong aversion, for example, from great difficulties at school.

Letters to clients

White and Epston's (1990) book is still a great source of ideas on writing letters to both adults and children. There are many types of possible letters, but here I will outline only a selection.

Letters concerning trauma

These letters were discussed in Chapter 22. In essence, they can be a summary of what the person has suffered, but also move on to a consideration of strengths.

Letters summarizing solutions

A very useful and simple letter is one written to summarize and state clearly ideas for coping or change that were discussed in the session. They can be done at any stage of therapy: the following is an example.

Dear Susan

We discussed this week what helps at the moment with your drinking. You said things go better if you sit with the others watching TV in the evening, and not sit alone in another room.
You also mentioned that reading helps to take your mind off negative thinking.

Yours sincerely

Letters of encouragement

Dear Daniel

You told me this week that for the first time you had managed to go swimming and refused to hide your body from others.
I thought that was an important step and took a lot of courage.

All the best

Writing by clients

Writing by clients can take many forms. Clients can be asked to fill in answers to one or two written questions, but at the other extreme can be asked to write what can amount to an autobiography.

One useful and simple question sheet is to ask clients:

- Write about any difficulties that occur this week.
- What are your thoughts and feelings about these events?

This type of writing might be used to begin to describe and understand a repetitive problem.

The client can also be asked to focus on coping:

- Notice this week how you overcame the urge to … (fight, criticize yourself, etc.).

Complex narrative of life

Mahoney (2003) described an approach called 'life review': the client is asked to review all or most of their life. Alternatively, a person can be asked to describe what was happening by focusing on specific years or on other useful units, such as 'your 20s', writing a few paragraphs for every time period. Another version is to ask clients to:

- Write about what has been important in your life.
- Consider how these things have influenced you.

Roberts (1999) has described compiling the story of a person's life in the context of long-term psychiatric rehabilitation. The aim of such work is often to restore to a person a sense of the past and restore identity in a context where it has been lost or eroded. A small number of clients explicitly ask to understand their lives better, and life review can be used for this purpose.

Documents

Formal letters written to other professionals, but copied to a client, can also be useful. One client received such a letter written by a therapist I supervised: the client told the therapist that now she really did believe what the therapist had been saying to her, that is, that she had shown resilience and coping. Rarely is saying something once in therapy going to be enough: rather, a new idea or narrative will need multiple reminders.

Overview

It is very useful to augment therapy with expressive modes: visualizing, enactment and writing are particularly useful approaches. They invite the imagination to build something and are ways of increasing confidence and of promoting growth through small steps.

28

Living with emotions

Many clients not only have powerful negative emotions but respond to emotions in destructive ways. A client might feel fear, and then attack themselves for being fearful, and subsequently drink excessive alcohol to numb these bad feelings. It is also likely that those who suffered a difficult childhood are left with long-term extreme reactivity, that is, they feel highly upset and destabilized when negative events occur and this reaction is easily triggered (Gerhardt, 2004).

Whilst working with emotional difficulties has been important for those working with personality disorders (Linehan, 1993), variations of these methods are now used with many conditions (Berking et al., 2008). Working with emotion was also, of course, the central concern of Rogers' (1951) therapy and likewise is central in the constructivist approach of Greenberg (2002). Greenberg in his work gives a key role to finding expression, narratives, and understanding the origin of emotions.

Individual and group work for emotions

The following approach can be used in one-to-one sessions or in a group format. In general I think it most useful to combine the client's individual therapy with groups for working with emotions, particularly for those with extreme difficulties such as psychotic clients. Sessions can be given in a limited number, about ten, but it can be useful to present the work as a rolling programme.

Berking et al. (2008) identified eight skills as being the most useful for coping with emotions:

1. Calm breathing;
2. Muscle relaxation exercises;
3. Developing self-compassion;
4. Remembering one's strengths;
5. Focusing attention on what is felt in order to put emotions into words or images;
6. Taking up an attitude of acceptance;
7. Working out what started the emotion;
8. Thinking of ways of changing the situation that might have started the emotion or finding any way of inducing a new emotion.

Most of the above are readily understand by clients and can be put into practice by standard CBT skills. For the following skill areas, however, I find narrative and constructivist ideas particularly useful.

Appreciation

Clients with extreme difficulties find the idea of strengths very challenging: as an alternative, drawing on an idea by de Shazer (1988), the idea of 'appreciation', of finding what is valuable, can be given.

Appreciating your life

You might not like the idea of 'strengths'. That it is somehow too much.

As an alternative, it can be useful to think instead of appreciating what is of value in your life right now, about people you know, yourself, things you have or do, whatever it is.

You can also appreciate the very moment now, the very simple things of life: good weather, a walk in the park, a beautiful plant on your window ledge.

How to practise

Think now of anything you can appreciate about your day. Has something gone well in spite of all the difficulties? Has someone been helpful? You might try this practice before thinking about difficult emotions, or as a way of coping in a difficult time.

Understanding onset and thinking of change

The skill of understanding is also very difficult, and the method I have found most helpful involves giving out the following narrative-based idea.

Understanding emotions using narrative

If you are distressed, the following can be helpful to understand what has happened and why. It is helpful if you can write down the following:

- *Think of when the feeling started.*
- *Describe what was happening before the main feeling and how it developed.*
- *Think of what was happening around you and inside you.*
- *What does this event mean to you?*

Does any metaphor or image help express how this situation felt? What would you compare it to? (It felt like... or I felt like...)
What happened after the main event?
How did you deal with your feelings?

Reflecting on the episode
Re-read your writing and consider: were your feelings mainly about what happened there and then, or are your feelings mainly about things that happened to you in your past?

Having written a narrative, or at least thought about the events, the client is then asked to make a classification of the emotion as either having been triggered by some obvious event or appearing to have come 'out the blue', to have started with no obvious cause. This is a simplified version of Greenberg's classification. It is then explained that the latter sort of emotion could link to things from the past, or that it is a sort of habit of feeling developed over years.

To work with emotions, clients can also use metaphors and images in the attempt to put them into words (see Chapters 18 and 27) and use solution-focused questions to prepare lists of what has worked in the past to help. For further ideas on working with emotions, Greenberg (2002) is an excellent resource.

29

Depression

In this chapter I shall sketch an approach for working with complex depressions, that is, manifestations of depression that are quite severe in intensity, long-standing or chronic, and usually accompanied by diverse types of comorbid symptoms and/or long-term social or emotional problems. The approach is, therefore, not intended for first-onset mild depression, nor, at the other extreme, depression comorbid with personality disorders which might require dialectical behaviour therapy or schema therapy. Working in a secondary care service, such as a community mental health team, complex depressions are quite common.

Sequence of therapy

A useful sequence for working with depression is as follows:

1. Exploration of present symptoms; what are these like for this person?
2. Tracing the history of the symptoms and/or other accompanying difficulties;
3. Attempting to understand these difficulties as they occurred over time in context and how they contribute to the present;
4. Solution-focused work on coping with symptoms such as rumination and the encouragement of positive activities the person enjoys, activity scheduling, attention to regulating food and sleep;
5. An attempt to understand the main problems that triggered and maintain the depression and doing therapy as appropriate. This usually involves an articulation of the old way of living versus a new narrative suggesting ways forward and a different way of living;

6. Exploration of goals, values and motives;
7. An extended focus on being constructional, putting into action all the things which work; finding ways of promoting and activating positive aspects of the dispositional self.

Assessment

As stated in Chapter 16, before doing a full narrative assessment, it is useful to discuss with the client issues such as:

- The actual symptoms;
- Attitude to therapy;
- An outline of recent events and present life circumstances;
- A simple overview of adult and child years.

This might take one session and then is followed by the mutual decision to proceed or not. Given an agreement to proceed, the following should be explored.

First, the 'phenomenology' of depression for this person is examined. What is depression for this person, what are its components?

- What is depression like for you?
- How has it affected your life, self, relationships?
- When is it worse? What is it like then? Does it change over time?

When clients have given their descriptions, it can then be useful to consider specific features, such as:

- Do you sometimes feel empty?
- Do you feel alone, cut off from others?
- Do you feel that life is 'over', 'suspended', that it happens for others and not for you?
- Do you 'ruminate' or engage in spirals of negative thoughts?
- Have you moments of explosive emotions or very difficult feelings?

These features are drawn from several sources, such as classic textbooks of depression (Beck, 1967), but they also draw on the tradition of qualitative research, such as Karp (1996), Ridge (2009), Rhodes and Smith (2010), Smith and Rhodes (in press). I think it helps to learn about the presentation of depression from several sources: it is not enough to rely on the *Diagnostic and Statistical Manual of Mental Disorders* (DSM) list of symptoms, nor, I believe, basic CBT books on depression.

The next essential area to explore is the person's present situation and ongoing problems and struggles of life.

- What does the person see as the main contributions to their depression, or what is upsetting and disturbing the client?

  Some common areas are:

- Interpersonal difficulties;
- Long-term effects of trauma;
- Ongoing social destruction and its effects on the person's existence, for example, as found in refugees.

Conceptualization

After this initial exploration, it can be useful for the therapist to build an integrated narrative account of these diverse features. This offers an explanation of why the person might be depressed. In general, I think this is best done as a dialogue with the person. For an illustration, see Sally in Chapter 19. The conceptualization is added to as the work evolves.

Solution-focused coping

The aim of this phase is to find what can help the person deal with the specific processes of depression, in particular:

- Ruminations and excessive thinking;
- Poor sleep, eating, exercise;
- Excessive withdrawal and inactivity;
- Emotional outbursts;
- Any destructive habits such as alcohol misuse.

From such a list, one can select 'easier' areas to discuss now, emphasizing that the difficult areas come later. If not mentioned, it can be useful to ask explicitly, for example about rumination, and then explore what works to stop that. Where possible, it is helpful to refer to groups focused on skills such as mindfulness or emotion coping.

Core problems and new ways of living

The exact therapy needed for the client depends on the unique cluster of long-term difficulties:

- If the client reports serious interpersonal conflict and upset, then a weekly narrative interaction focus (see Chapter 25) may be appropriate;
- If the person shows long-term trauma, then narrative exposure work (see Chapter 22);
- If there are issues of ruptured life flow or of existential problems, then this could involve both trauma work and work on identity, values and motivations (see Chapter 24).

Whatever the life problem, coming out of depression requires a new narrative of self and life, and also that changes are made in the way a person lives and in the person's actual lived world.

Relapse prevention and recovery

Research suggests many depressions are chronic, and many who have been treated for depression relapse. It is helpful to discuss this with clients, and for some, actually to analyse the warning signs of relapse and how to cope. Ridge (2009), using indepth interviewing, explored what clients themselves say about coping and recovery: they emphasized professionals and general practitioners having an understanding attitude, various types of therapy and a range of self-help and care methods.

Sally: Overview

Sally has been discussed in several chapters. The issues which entrenched her in depression were self-hate and self-disgust, combined with memories of abuse. The work followed this sequence:

- SF work revealing how she looked after her son very well and memories of a good family;
- Trauma narration concerning her sister's death and years of domestic violence;
- Building a non-blaming new narration of how the abuser had exploited her;
- Continuing to try to live according to her deepest values of caring for her son;
- Work on recurrent imagery of being attacked when out;
- A continuous mapping of living according to 'self-hate' versus living according to ideas of 'care', of commitment and having a 'good heart' (added later), creating an intergenerational story of care, of passing on an attitude of dedication.

The frame of self-hate versus living with a good heart, and later adding kind but strong, like her father, was very useful in the long term for changing Sally's way of life. Slowly she moved out of depression and resisted self-hate attacks.

Conclusion

Depression, I believe, is most often a response to the world: what matters to the person (love, work, family life, hopes for the future) has been destroyed or is in continuous danger. This seems to have the effect of 'emptying' the person of the very capacity to be motivated, and in particular to pursue those aims and values which have been central to a person's identity and sense of self. In severe cases the person turns on themselves with insults and attacks.

In reactive depression the destruction is new, but for chronic depression the destruction of the person's world, and usually attacks on the self, continues over years. Sometimes the reality of the person's life has not changed, or alternatively, the person is stuck in repetitive patterns of self-attack, difficult interactions and avoidance. To move out of depression the person needs a new way of living and new narration involving hope.

30

Diverse applications: OCD and refugees

In this chapter I will explore how NCBT, and related ideas, have been developed and applied in two specific disorders.

The inference-based approach to OCD

O'Connor and associates (2006, 2009) suggest in their analysis of obsessive-compulsive disorder (OCD) that core ingredients are the generation of a 'bridging narrative' containing remote and usually extravagant possibilities of what might or could happen, and, directly linked to this, doubt or mistrust concerning the senses or nature of the self. Clients are engaging in a sort of inference, a way of thinking, and not just responding to intrusions. They generate extravagant stories of what might have occurred and are overcome by the persuasive nature of what is imagined in narrative form.

From the viewpoint of this book, the work of O'Connor is a fascinating example showing how narrative can contribute to pathology, but also how lack of trust in the everyday world makes a distinctive contribution.

The following example illustrates their concepts:

- Sense information: 'The food looks clean ... but maybe...'
- Story (bridging narrative): 'There are germs on all surfaces and some are deadly and not killed by cooking. Many things touched this food. Perhaps someone came along just now and touched both surfaces when I was out of the room.'
- Obsessive inference: 'So maybe this food is contaminated even if it looks clean and was cooked.'

A patient can have several different obsessions: however, when all these different obsessions are analysed, O'Connor suggests these often all relate to a 'vulnerable self theme', that is, the person fears becoming, for example, the kind of person who allows harm to happen.

The inference-based treatment has several phases. The patterns of doubt and bridging narrative are analysed. A major aim then is to educate the client about 'authentic doubt', for example, where there is new real 'sensory information' (such as the smell of burning), in contrast to obsessional doubt, which is not linked to new information about the environment. To counter the bridging narrative, an alternative realistic narrative is elaborated, with the aim of 'grounding the person in reality sensing'.

O'Connor and associates suggest their work may have applications in other areas where there is an aspect of obsessionality, such as eating disorders and body dysmorphia.

Refugees and psychotic features

London has many refugees fleeing torture, war and major upheavals. For some, narrative exposure therapy or standard posttraumatic stress disorder treatments are appropriate. Some, however, have complex presentations in that they show features of rather extreme emotional chaos, and some have psychotic features (Parrett et al., 2013, in press).

It is my clinical observation that these psychotic features are often not like the ones normally found in persons diagnosed as having schizophrenia. Many mention 'voices' directly linked to persecutors, and the person wavers on whether these are real or not.

I have used NCBT with several such clients, adapting it to specific unique needs. The work tends to involve the following elements:

- A brief overview of the person's situation and history;
- A determined effort to focus on solutions for coping. There is sometimes an aspect of self-harm, and this needs to be addressed;

- Over time there is a shift to exploring the narrative of trauma. For some clients it can also be very helpful to write out their life story;
- There is a continuous focus on exploring values and future life goals. A central problem is the loss of meaning, loss of connection to others and loss of purpose in life. One approach is to think deeply about what those who have died might have wished for the person's life. This takes inspiration from White's (1989) work on rebuilding a relationship with the dead person;
- As there is a movement to reinvigorating lost values, plans and choosing life, re-engagement in the world is explored.

Case illustration

One client lost three of his family and was tortured himself. He was overcome by grief and attacked himself for not saving the others and for being what he perceived as 'weak'. He was depressed, flooded with negative memories and engaged in chaotic and dangerous behaviours. His emotions were subject to extreme fluctuations.

We worked on several areas, and had to switch focus as appropriate. There were many elements: exploring grief and the expression of agony in the session by bringing his poetry and writing to the session; the construction of an autobiography; repeated examination of how he alone could not stop a government and a focus on how he could live now and in the future. In one early phase, after some stabilization, a report for the Home Office was needed and for this the general history of his imprisonment and some episodes of torture were explored in our sessions and documented. The work could not have been carried out without the help of one interpreter throughout, who became a sort of co-therapist and advisor on cultural issues that arose at several points.

Many direct suggestions were given about changing potentially harmful behaviours; for example, he had the habit of taking sleeping pills in the day with, of course, very negative effects. The issue of the client being in control, however, was emphasized; that is, it was 'his life', he must 'choose', but this is what we think.

For a very long time he had no hope at all. He was extremely negative about life and saw little reason to live. One day he saw a child hurt in an accident and came to the session very upset. By exploring why he thought the accident terrible (that is, using ideas from White on evaluating a person's reaction to something negative), I was able to find out that he still held on to certain values such that it was wrong for this child to suffer and therefore he saw that he did in fact still care about some things. He had other negative reactions to events which allowed further exploration of his values: these opened up discussions about what he had hoped for before all these terrible events and the values his father had stood for.

With a client like this, it could be said that many process-orientated techniques might also have been useful, for example, meditation, but the challenge here was that this client would not do anything remotely useful for himself until he began to choose to live, and this was only achieved by a focus on meaning, on what had happened, and on what the dead would think, and imagining a future and engaging in purpose. For many clients there is a great need for work with both content and process: the two cannot be separated.

Overview

NCBT has, I believe, many uses, and several types, but it seems particularly appropriate for certain sorts of complex case where there are continued effects of a difficult past and a need for developing present coping and a more encouraging picture of the future.

The topics of narrative, metaphor, meaningful action, dispositional behaviours, certainty, trust and confidence might however be relevant to many human concerns. They are essential for understanding presenting problems and are key features of therapeutic practice.

References

Adenauer, H., Catani, C., Gola, H., Keil, J., Ruf, M., Schuer, M. & Neuner, F. (2011). Narrative exposure therapy for PTSD increases top-down processing of aversive stimuli – evidence from a randomized controlled treament trial. *Neuroscience,* 12, 127.

Arciero, G. & Bondolfi, G. (2011). *Selfhood, Identity, and Personality Styles.* Chichester: Wiley.

Bannick, F. (2012). *Practising Positive CBT: From Reducing Distress to Building Success.* Chichester: Wiley-Blackwell.

Bargh, J.A. (2005). Bypassing the will: toward demystifying the nonconscious control of social behaviour. In R.R. Hassin, J.S. Uleman & J.A. Bargh (Eds.), *The New Unconscious.* Oxford: OUP.

Baumeister, R.F. (2005). *The Cultural Animal: Human Nature, Meaning and Social Life.* Oxford: Oxford University Press.

Beck, A.T. (1967). *Depression: Clinical, Experimental, and Theoretical Aspects.* New York: Harper and Row.

Beck, A.T. (1995). Beyond belief: A theory of modes, personality, and psychopathology. In P.M. Salvoskis (Ed.), *Frontiers of Cognitive Therapy.* New York: Guilford.

Berking, M., Wupperman, P., Reichardt, A., Pejic, T., Dippel, A. & Znoj, H. (2008). Emotion-regulation skills as a treatment target in psychotherapy. *Behaviour Research and Therapy*, 46, 1230–1237.

Blenkiron, P. (2010). *Stories and Analogies in Cognitive Therapy.* Chichester: Wiley.

Bliss, E.V. & Bray, D. (2009). The smallest solution focused particles: towards a minimalist definition of when therapy is solution focused. *Journal of Systemic Therapies*, 28, 62–74.

Bourdieu, P. (1990). *The Logic of Practice*. Cambridge: Polity Press.

Bowlby, J. (1969). *Attachment and Loss. vol. 1: Attachment*. London: Hogarth Press.

Brewin, C.R. (2006). Understanding cognitive behaviour therapy: A retrieval competition account. *Behaviour Research and Therapy*, 44, 6, 765–784.

Brewin, C.R. & Power, M.J (1999). Integrating psychological therapies: processes of meaning transformation. *British Journal of Medical Psychology*, 72, 143–157.

Bruner, J. (1986). *Actual Minds, Possible Worlds*. Cambridge: Harvard University Press.

Butler, G., Fennell, M. & Hackmann, A. (2008). *Cognitive Behavioural Therapy for Anxiety Disorders*. New York: Guilford.

Cienfuegos, J. & Monelli, C. (1983). The testimony of political repression as a therapeutic instrument. *American Journal of Orthopsychiatry*, 53, 43–51.

Cooper, M. (2003). *Existential Therapies*. London: Sage.

Cox, M. & Theilgaard, A. (1987). *Mutative Metaphors in Psychology*. London: Tavistock Publications.

Cozolino, L. J. (2010). *The Neuroscience of Psychotherapy: Healing the Social Brain*, 2nd edn. New York: Norton.

Dallos, R. (2006). *Attachment Narrative Therapy: Integrating Narrative, Systemic and Attachment Therapies*. Maidenhead: Open University Press.

Damasio, A. (1999). *The Feeling of What Happens*. San Diego: Harcourt.

de Shazer, S. (1985). *Keys to Solution in Brief Therapy*. New York: Norton.

de Shazer, S. (1988). *Clues: Investigating Solutions in Brief Therapy*. New York: Norton.

Dryden, W. (Ed.) (2012). *Cognitive Behaviour Therapies*. London: Sage.

Ehlers, A. & Clark, D.M. (2000). A cognitive model of posttraumatic stress disorder. *Behaviour Research and Therapy*, 38, 319–345.

Eron, J.B. & Lund, T.W. (1996). *Narrative Solutions in Brief Therapy*. New York: Guilford.

Fauconnier, G. & Turner, M. (2002). *The Way We Think: Conceptual Blending and the Mind's Hidden Complexities*. New York: Basic Books.

Gallagher, S. (2007). Pathologies in narrative structure. In D.D Hutto (Ed.), *Narrative and Understanding Persons*. Cambridge: CUP.

Gallagher, S. & Zahavi, D. (2008). *The Phenomenological Mind*. London: Routledge.

Gerhardt, S. (2004). *Why Love Matters: How Affection Shapes a Baby's Brain*. London: Routledge.

Gilbert, P. (1989). *Human Nature and Suffering.* Hove: Lawrence Erlbaum Associates.

Gilbert, P. (2010). *Compassion Focused Therapy.* Hove: Routledge.

Gingerich, W.J. & Eisengart, S. (2000). Solution-focused brief therapy: A review of the outcome research. *Family Process*, 39, 477–498.

Goldie, P. (2000). *The Emotions: A Philosophical Exploration.* Oxford: Oxford University Press.

Goldie, P. (2004). *On Personality.* London: Routledge

Gollwitzer, P.M., Bayer, U.C. & McCulloch, K.C. (2005). The control of the unwanted. In R.R. Hassin, J.S. Uleman, J.A. Bargh (Eds.), *The New Unconscious*. Oxford: OUP.

Gonçalves, O.F. (1994). Cognitve narrative psychotherapy: the hermeneutic construction of alternative meanings. *Journal of Cognitive Psychotherapy,* 8, 2, 105–123.

Greenberg, L.S. (2002). *Emotion-Focused Therapy.* Washington: APA.

Griffin, M. (2003). Narrative behaviour therapy? *Australian and New Zealand Journal of Family Therapy*, 24, 1, 33–37.

Guidano, V.F. (1991). *The Self in Process.* New York: Guilford Press.

Guidano, V.F. & Liotti, G. (1983). *Cognitive Processes and Emotional Disorders.* New York: Guilford.

Hackmann, A., Bennett-Levy, J. & Holmes, E.A. (2011). *Oxford Guide to Imagery in Cognitive Therapy.* Oxford: OUP.

Hall, P.L. & Tarrier, N. (2003). The cognitive-behavioural treatment of low self-esteem in psychotic patients: a pilot study. *Behaviour Research and Therapy,* 41, 317–332.

Hallam, R.S. & O'Connor, K.P. (2002). A dialogical approach to obsessions. *Psychology and Psychotherapy: Theory, Research and Practice,* 75, 333–348.

Harré, R. (1979). *Social Being: A Theory for Social Psychology.* Oxford: Basil Blackwell.

Herman, J. (1992). *Trauma and Recovery.* New York: Basic Books.

Hutto, D.D. (2008). *Folk Psychological Narratives: The Sociocultural Basis of Understanding Reasons.* Cambridge, MA: Bradford.

Jakes, S. & Rhodes, J. (2003). The effect of different components of psychological therapy on people with delusions: five experimental single case. *Clinical Psychology and Psychotherapy*, 10, 302–315.

Jakes, S., Rhodes, J. & Turner, T. (1999). Effectiveness of cognitive therapy for delusions in routine practice. *British Journal of Psychiatry,* 175, 331–335.

Karp, A.D. (1996). Spea*king of Sadness: Depression, Disconnection and the Meanings of Illness.* New York: OUP.

Kashima, J. (1997). Culture, narrative, and human motivation. In D. Munro, J. Schumaker, & S.C. Carr (Eds.), *Motivation and Culture*. New York: Rutledge.

Kelly, G.A. (1955). *The Psychology of Personal Constructs,* vols 1 and 2. New York: Norton.

Korrelboom, K., Marissen, M. & van Assendelft, T. (2010). Competitive memory training (COMET) for low self-esteem in patients with personality disorders: a randomized effectiveness study. *Behavioural and Cognitive Psychotherapy,* 39, 1–19.

Kuyken, W., Padesky, C.A. & Dudely, R. (2009). *Collaborative Case Conceptualization.* New York: Guilford.

Lakoff, G (1987). *Women, Fire, and Dangerous Things. What Categories Reveal About the Mind.* Chigaco: University of Chicago Press.

Lakoff, G. & Johnson, M. (1980). *Metaphors We Live By.* Chicago: University of Chicago Press.

Lee, D.A. (2005). The perfect nurturer: A model to develop a compassionate mind within the context of cognitive therapy. In P Gilbert (Ed.), *Compassion: Conceptualisations, Research, and Use in Psychotherapy.* Hove: Routledge.

LeDoux, J. (1998). *The Emotional Brain.* London: Weidenfeld and Nicolson.

Linehan, M.M. (1993). *Cognitive-Behavioral Treatment of Borderline Personality Disorder.* New York: Guilford Press.

Lipchik, E. (2002). *Beyond Technique in Solution Focused Therapy.* New York: Guilford Press.

Løgstrup, K.E. (1956/1997). *The Ethical Demand.* Notre Dame: University of Notre Dame.

MacIntyre, A. (1981). *After Virtue: A Study in Moral Theory.* London: Duckworth.

MacLeod, A.K. & Moore, R. (2000). Positive thinking revisited: positive cognitions, well-being, and mental health. *Clinical Psychology and Psychotherapy,* 7, 1–10.

Mahoney, M.J. (1991). *Human Change Processes.* New York: Basic Books.

Mahoney, M.J. (2003). *Constructive Psychotherapy: A Practical Guide.* New York: Guilford Press.

Martell, C.R., Addis, M.E. & Jacobson, N.S. (2001). *Depression in Context: Strategies for Guided Action.* New York: Norton.

Maslow, A.H. (1968). *Toward a Psychology of Being.* New York: Van Nostrand.

McAdams, D. (1993). *Stories We Live By: Personal Myths and the Making of the Self.* New York: Guilford Press.

McCullough, J.P. (2000). *Treatment for Chronic Depression: Cognitive Behavioural Analysis System of Psychotherapy.* New York: Guilford Press.

Meichenbaum, D. (1993). Changing conceptions of cognitive behaviour modification: retrospect and prospect. *Journal of Consulting and Clinical Psychology*, 61, 2, 202–204.

Meichenbaum, D. (1994). *A Clinical Handbook/Practical Therapist Manual for Treating PTSD*. Ontario: Institute Press.

Moyal-Sharrock, D. (2007). *Understanding Wittgenstein's On Certainty*. Basingstoke: Palgrave Macmillan.

Morgan, A.M. (2000). *What is Narrative Therapy?* Adelaide: Dulwich Centre.

Neuner, F., Schauer, M., Roth, W.T. & Elbert, T. (2002). A narrative exposure treatment as intervention in a refugee camp: a case report. *Behavioural and Cognitive Psychotherapy*, 30, 205–209.

O'Connor, K.P., Aardema, F. & Pelissier, M-C. (2006). *Beyond Reasonable Doubt: Reasoning Process in Obsessive-Compulsive Disorder and Related Disorders*. Chichester: Wiley.

O'Connor, K.P., Koszegi, N., Aardema, F., van Niekerk, J. & Taillon, A. (2009). An inference-based approach to treating obsessive-compulsive disorders. *Cognitive and Behavioural Practice*, 16, 420–429.

O'Nell, T.D. (1999). "Coming home" among Northern Plains Vietnam veterans: psychological transformations in pragmatic perspective. *Ethos*, 27, 4, 441–465.

Padesky, C.A. (1994). Schema change processes in cognitive therapy. *Clinical Psychology and Psychotherapy*, 1 (5), 267–278.

Parrett, N.S., Rhodes, J.E. & Mason, O. (2013). A qualitative study of refugees with psychotic symptoms (in press).

Pennebaker, J.W. (1990). *Opening Up: The Healing Power of Confiding in Others*. New York: Guilford Press.

Phelps, E.A. (2005). The interaction of emotion and cognition: the relation between the human amygdala and cognitive awareness. In R.R. Hassin, J.S. Uleman, J.A.Bargh (Eds.), *The New Unconscious*. Oxford: OUP.

Postma, K. & Rao, N. (2006). Using solution-focused questioning to facilitate the process of change in cognitive behavioural therapy for food neophobia in adults. *Behavioural and Cognitive Psychotherapy*, 34, 3, 371–375.

Prinz, W. (2003). How do we know about our own actions? In S. Maasen, W. Prinz & G. Roth (Eds.), *Voluntary Action: Brains, Minds, and Sociality*. New York: OUP.

Ramsay, J.R. (1998). Postmodern cognitive therapy: cognitions, narratives, and personal meaning-making. *Journal of Cognitive Psychotherapy*, 12, 1, 39–55.

Ratcliffe, M. (2007). *Rethinking Common Sense Psychology*. Basingstoke: Palgrave Macmillan.

Ratcliffe, M. (2008). *Feelings of Being: Phenomenology, Psychiatry and the Sense of Reality.* Oxford: OUP.

Ratcliffe, M. (2010). Depression, guilt and emotional depth. *Inquiry,* 53, 6, 602–628.

Ratcliffe, M. (2013). The structure of interpersonal experience. In D. Moran & R. Jensen, (Eds.), *Phenomenology of Embodied Subjectivity.* Dordrecht: Springer (in press).

Ratner, H., George, E. & Iveson, C. (2012). *Solution Focused Brief Therapy: 100 Key Points and Techniques.* London: Routledge.

Read, J., Mosher, L. R. & Bentall, R. P. (Eds.) (2004). *Models of Madness.* Hove: Brunner-Routledge.

Rhodes, J. & Gipps, R. (2008). Delusions, certainty, and the background. *Philosophy, Psychiatry, and Psychology,* 15, 4, 295–310.

Rhodes, J. & Jakes, S. (2002). Using solution focused therapy during a psychotic crisis: a case study. *Clinical Psychology and Psychotherapy,* 9, 139–148.

Rhodes, J. & Jakes, S. (2004). The contribution of metaphor and metonymy to delusions. *Psychology and Psychotherapy: Theory, Research, and Practice,* 73, 211–225.

Rhodes, J. & Jakes, S. (2009). *Narrative CBT for Psychosis.* Hove: Routledge.

Rhodes, J. & Jakes, S. (2010). Perspectives on the onset of delusions. *Clinical Psychology and Psychotherapy,* 17, 2, 136–146.

Rhodes, J. & Smith, J.A. (2010). "The top of my head came off": a phenomenological interpretative analysis of the experience of depression. *Counselling Psychology Quarterly.* 23, 4, 399–409.

Ricoeur, P. (1984). *Time and Narrative,* vol. 1. Chicago: UCP.

Ridge, D. (2009). *Recovery from Depression: Using the Narrative Approach.* London: Jessica Kingsley.

Roberts, G. (1999). Healing stories. In G. Roberts & J. Holmes, (Eds.), *Narrative in Psychiatry and Psychotherapy.* Oxford: Oxford University Press.

Rogers, C.R. (1951). *Client-centered Therapy: Its Current Practice, Implications and Theory.* Oxford: Houghton Mifflin.

Rowan, T. & O'Hanlon, W. (1999). *Solution-Orientated Therapy for Chronic and Severe Mental Illness.* New York: Wiley.

Russell, R.L. (1991). Narrative in views of humanity, science, and action: lessons for cognitive therapy. *Journal of Cognitive Psychotherapy,* 5, 4, 241–256.

Ryle, A. & Kerr, I.B. (2002). *Introducing Cognitive Analytic Therapy.* Chichester: Wiley.

Sarbin, T. (1986). The narrative as a root metaphor for psychology. In T.R. Sarbin (Ed.) *Narrative Psychology: The Storied Nature of Human Conduct.* New York: Praeger.

Schacter, L.D. (1996). *Searching for Memory.* New York: Basic Books.

Searle, J.R. (1983). *Intentionality: An essay in the Philosophy of Mind.* Cambridge: Cambridge University Press.

Searle, J.R. (1992). *The Rediscovery of the Mind.* Cambridge: MIT Press.

Siegle, D.J. (1999). *Developing Mind: Toward a Neurobiology of Interpersonal Experience.* New York: Guilford.

Sims, P.A. & Whynot, C.A. (1997). Hearing metaphor: an approach to working with family-generated metaphor. *Family Process,* 36, 341–355.

Smith, J. A. & Rhodes, J. (in press). Examining the experiential features of first-episode depression: a qualitative analysis.

Talvitie, V. & Tiitinen, H. (2006). From the repression of contents to the rules of the (narrative) self: a present-day cognitive view of the 'Freudian phenomenon' of repressed contents. *Psychology and Psychotherapy: Theory, Research and Practice*, 79, 164–181.

Trevarthan, C. & Aitken, K.J. (2001). Infant intersubjectivity: research, theory, and clinical applications. *Journal of Child Psychology and Psychiatry,* 42, 1, 3–48.

Turner, M. (1996). *The Literary Mind: The Origins of Thought and Language.* New York: Oxford University Press.

Vromans, L.P. & Schweitzer R.D. (2011). Narrative therapy for adults with major depressive disorder: improved symptom and interpersonal outcomes. *Psychotherapy Research,* 21, 1, 4–15.

White, M. (1989). *Selected Papers.* Adelaide: Dulwich Centre Publications.

White, M. (2007). *Maps of Narrative Practice.* New York: Norton.

White, M. & Epston, D. (1990). *Narrative Means to Therapeutic Ends.* New York: Norton.

Wilkinson, R. & Pickett, K. (2009). *The Sprit Level: Why Equality is Better for Everyone.* London: Penguin.

Winter, D.A. & Viney, L.L. (Eds.) (2005). *Personal Construct Psychotherapy: Advances in Theory, Practice and Research.* London: Whurr.

Wittgenstein, L. (1953). *Philosophical Investigations.* Oxford: Blackwell Publishers.

Wittgenstein, L. (1969). *On Certainty.* Oxford: Blackwell Publishers.

Young, E., Klosko, J.S. & Weishaar, M.E. (2003). *Schema Therapy: A Practitioner's Guide.* New York: Guilford Press.

Zahavi, D. (2007). Self and other: the limits of narrative understanding. In D.D Hutto, (Ed.), *Narrative and Understanding Persons.* Cambridge: CUP.

Index